It's rare to find someone who can talk about the call of Jesus on our lives in a way that doesn't feel burdensome. Jason Mitchell has attained that balance. In *No Easy Jesus*, you will get the sense that Jason is on the journey of following right along with you. He will challenge you without weighing you down. He will inspire you to take Jesus up on the two-word invitation that he's been extending for centuries: "Follow me." My prayer for you is that you will read these pages and be inspired to follow Jesus with more passion and greater joy.

KYLE IDLEMAN
Author of *Not a Fan* and *Grace Is Greater*

No Easy Jesus offers a spring for the thirsty soul. For anyone struggling with faith, church, or life, this book offers a gritty yet inspiring look at what it means to follow Jesus. You need to read this book.

MARGARET FEINBERG
Author of *Fight Back with Joy*

Nothing great is ever easy. We know this, and yet when it comes to matters of faith, we lose hope when the way is not easy. *No Easy Jesus* helps us reconcile the hurts, fears, and challenges of life with the true fullness of life in Christ. Read this one!

JENNI CATRON
Author of *The 4 Dimensions of Extraordinary Leadership*

No Easy Jesus is a simple book about the hard call to follow Jesus. Through powerful stories and memorable sayings, Jason Mitchell shares the tension between the uncomplicated yet uncompromising invitation that Jesus offers to all of us. It is an easy thing to raise a hand, walk forward in a service, or sign a decision card, but it is a hard thing to follow Jesus every day. However, Jason reminds us that Jesus is right there with us on the journey.

CALEB KALTENBACH
Author of *Messy Grace*

In a style that is both raw and gritty, Jason Mitchell leaves behind the typical hollow slogans we are often fed and instead offers up advice that will lead to true life change. Strikingly transparent and honest, Jason shares from his own personal experiences as well as from the experiences of those he has traveled with through life as a pastor, leader, and friend. Don't let this entertaining book fool you— intertwined in the stories is the challenge to live the life of following Jesus that will bring true transformation.

DAVID ASHCRAFT
Senior pastor, LCBC Church

NO
EASY
JESUS

HOW THE TOUGHEST CHOICES
LEAD TO THE GREATEST LIFE

JASON MITCHELL

TYNDALE
MOMENTUM™

The nonfiction imprint of
Tyndale House Publishers, Inc.

Visit Tyndale Momentum online at www.tyndalemomentum.com.

TYNDALE, Tyndale Momentum, and Tyndale's quill logo are registered trademarks of Tyndale House Publishers, Inc. Tyndale Momentum is the nonfiction imprint of Tyndale House Publishers, Inc., Carol Stream, Illinois.

No Easy Jesus: How the Toughest Choices Lead to the Greatest Life

Designed by Daniel Farrell

Published in association with literary agent Don Gates of The Gates Group, www.the -gates-group.com.

Names and other identifying details of some individuals have been changed to protect their privacy.

For information about special discounts for bulk purchases, please contact Tyndale House Publishers at csresponse@tyndale.com or call 800-323-9400.

Library of Congress Cataloging-in-Publication Data

Printed in the United States of America

23	22	21	20	19	18	17
7	6	5	4	3	2	1

For Jenny

No one has shown me what it looks like

to follow Jesus more than you have.

You pursue when others would run.

You open up when others would close down.

You give when others would grab.

You love when others would leave.

You are resilient and strong and beautiful in every way.

Thank you for refusing to settle for what's easiest

when what's best is out there for the taking.

CONTENTS

FOREWORD
BY KYLE IDLEMAN

HERE'S WHAT I BELIEVE about belief: People can believe they believe something that they may not actually believe.

Do you believe that's true?

Need a few examples?

Let me ask you some questions about what you believe:

- *Do you believe it's important to eat right and exercise?*
- *Do you believe that spending time with your family should be a high priority?*
- *Do you believe that saving money is something you should do?*

I don't need to hand out an official survey to know what percentage of Americans would say they believe those things are important. Almost everyone would say they agree that they hold those beliefs, and yet survey after survey indicates that those beliefs have little bearing on how people actually live.

- *I believe that eating right and exercising are vital, but the appetizers are two-for-one today, and the gym is too far away.*
- *I believe that spending time with my family is most important, but I just accepted a promotion that requires me to work evenings and weekends.*
- *I believe that saving money is necessary, but I just went into more debt to upgrade to a newer vehicle.*

A few years ago, I read an article by a psychiatrist who revealed that some of his patients believed things that had no basis in reality. One patient believed he could fly. Another patient was convinced she had been switched at birth and was actually part of the English royal family. Her belief was so genuine that she had developed a British accent. What stood out to me as I read the article was that the psychiatrist didn't use the word *beliefs* to describe these claims by his patients that had no basis in reality. The word he used was *delusions*. The truth is that beliefs that have no connection to reality, even if they're sincere, aren't beliefs at all; they're delusions.

If the reality of my life doesn't align with what I say I sincerely believe, then I need to step back and honestly ask myself whether I believe what I say I believe. Most of the frustration I have with myself comes when my behavior doesn't line up with my beliefs. That's especially true when it comes to my relationship with Jesus. I know that most Christians believe that they believe in Jesus, but belief is more than just intellectual acknowledgment or mental assent. The invitation Jesus offers is for us to *follow* him. Following Jesus is what happens when our lives align with what we say we believe about him.

It's rare to find someone who can talk about the call of Jesus on our lives in a way that doesn't feel burdensome. But Jason Mitchell has attained that balance in this book. It might be because he's so honest along the way. Throughout these pages, you will get the sense that Jason is on the journey of following right along with you. He gets personal, baring his soul in incredibly vulnerable ways at times. And it's that vulnerability that gives you the sense that you have a friend sharing his heart with you, cheering you on, saying, "Let's go after the life of Jesus together. I'm running after it, and I want a running partner."

This book will challenge you without weighing you down. It will inspire you to take Jesus up on the two-word invitation he's been extending for centuries: "Follow me." The invitation is to participate in the life of Christ, not to stand by passively and observe. My prayer for you is that you will read these pages and be inspired to follow Jesus with more passion and greater joy.

CHAPTER 1

JESUS ON A SHELF

I BOUGHT MYSELF a coloring book recently.

I can't believe I just told you that, but it's true. It's one of those coloring books that has intricately designed patterns on really nice paper, and it was labeled as an "advanced" coloring book, which helps me feel a little bit better about myself as I tell the story. But to be honest, I'm still kind of embarrassed about it.

It was an impulse purchase, pure and simple, brought on by a sudden fit of inspiration and nostalgia that hit me when I saw my son and daughter sitting at a table together coloring. When I was growing up, I loved coloring, sketching, and filling in the blank spaces on a page. I even won a coloring contest at Apple Tree Day Care when I was five. (My winning picture was a clown face, precisely executed with an assortment of primary colors.) But as much as I loved coloring when I was a kid, I thought my coloring book–buying days were decades behind me. But then there I was, at some crafty store that smelled like a shoemaker's workshop, spending money on an advanced coloring book—with an advanced marker set to go along with it.

You see, I started thinking about how much fun my wife, our two kids, and I would have together as we sat down by a warm fire every evening—each with a coloring book, laughing the entire time while drinking hot chocolate—and about all the places we could hang our creations around the house.

Of course, none of that ever happened. Instead, I used that advanced coloring book *once* . . . I think. And it has been sitting on one of our shelves—next to some really expensive markers—ever since.

I wish I could say this was the only time something like that has happened, but it's not. Over the years, I've accumulated countless items that have become monuments to passionate endeavors that never quite panned out. My shelves are crammed with books I started reading but never finished. I've become fascinated with certain topics for a moment—one time I really got into bees—only to set them aside and move on to the next thing. I have fishing gear collecting dust in the back corner of my garage. And I don't even want to admit how much money I've spent on other hobbies that never got off the ground.

Maybe you can relate.

Perhaps your garage or attic has become the permanent resting place for barely used golf clubs, a pile of unopened scrapbooking supplies, or a kayak that has rarely seen the water. And every time you walk by that guitar case, that blank canvas, or those gardening tools, you're reminded of what could've been. You're reminded that the passion you once had has faded or no longer exists.

The dust collecting on those things we were once so excited about reveals a fundamental truth about life: Passionate commitment without patient persistence leaves behind a graveyard of unfulfilled dreams.

What happens when the passion we felt early on in our relationship with God gives way to the humdrum of daily life? Where do we turn when the fire that once burned so brightly in our hearts becomes a barely visible ember? Hobbies that we never saw through to completion are one thing. At worst, we've wasted our time and money. But what happens when our faith and our hope get put up on a shelf next to the scrapbooking supplies? The potential consequences are much more severe—a wasted life.

This brings me to a dirty little secret that many of the bravest Christians I know have shared with me. Few dare to speak the words out loud, because it feels as if we're taking a slap at God—and it doesn't make *us* look all that great either. Yet it affects us painfully on the inside every single day.

Here it is: Believing in Jesus has left us disappointed.

Maybe for you it's more than *disappointed*—you feel

disillusioned, maybe even *cheated*. You expected something more from this whole following-Jesus thing. But it hasn't delivered.

At one point in your life, you were thrilled and hopeful about living a life of trusting in Jesus. But over time your experience has failed to live up to your expectations. Somewhere along the line, your relationship with Jesus lost its richness and intimacy.

Maybe you're discouraged because you feel helpless to make some needed changes in your life. Maybe your troubles feel unbearably hard—where is Jesus in all that? Maybe you haven't achieved the great things for God you once dreamed of. Instead, you're left feeling aimless and confused. You've waited—and *waited*—for your faith to make more of a difference. But it hasn't. And so you've begun to think, *This can't be all there is to the Christian life.*

If that's what you're thinking, here's the good news: You're right.

Jesus held out the promise of "a rich and satisfying life."[1] But for many of us, the truth is that *rich* and *satisfying* are the last words we would use to describe our current reality. I've felt this way in multiple seasons of my life. And as a pastor, I've heard countless people express the same disappointment to me in different ways.

In listening to story after story of people who have grown disappointed in their faith experience, I've noticed a few common threads: *discouragement*, *frustration*, and *boredom*. Let's see if one of these reasons helps you understand your own situation better.

It's for *Them*

Have you ever seen other Christians step boldly into risk-taking adventures and wondered, *How do they do that?* You hear stories of courage in the face of insurmountable obstacles. You see how these Christians respond with compassion and love, even when they are threatened or their patience is tested. In everything they do, they seem to ooze Jesus. Before long, you become acutely aware of the enormous gap between their intimacy with God and your own.

They must have something I don't have, you tell yourself. *They must know something I don't know.* Before long, disappointment sets in, and you start to believe that a life of deep and abiding faith in God—a life of passionate conviction—is a privilege reserved for someone else.

It's for the spiritually elite.

It's for the pastor.

It's for the ones who grew up in church.

It's for those who haven't made a wreck of their lives.

It's for the ones who have never struggled through addiction or seen the darker side of life.

To be honest, as discouraging as it is, we kind of *like* believing that a deep, abiding, life-altering faith is for the spiritually elite—because if that's true, we're absolved of our responsibility to pursue anything bigger than our present little lives. As Eugene Peterson says, "We are practiced in pleading inadequacy in order to avoid living at the best that God calls us to."[2]

Our discouragement in not being as far along as we

think we ought to be leads us to throw our hands in the air and "plead inadequacy." Instead of pressing in, we bow out; instead of moving forward, we shrink back. We settle for a small, safe life and a small, safe faith, because trusting, risking, and stepping out into bold acts of faith for God are for someone else. We accept the disappointing reality that our lives and our faith will never look like theirs.

If your discouragement doesn't come from everything you're *not* doing, then perhaps it stems from frustration over everything you *are* doing.

That's Just the Way It Is

Tell me if this pattern sounds familiar:

You say something, do something, or think something that you know isn't God's best for you.

You feel a certain level of conviction about it.

You go to God to confess, repent, and renew your resolve.

And then you find yourself doing it all over again the next day—or the next hour.

You try.

You fail.

Try again. Fail again.

Repeat.

If you live in that pattern long enough, it's easy to finally convince yourself that your temptations, struggles, sins, hang-ups, and habits are just the way things are—that nothing will ever change.

Sure, you still believe in Jesus, but you haven't experienced the power you need to move beyond the destructive patterns that seem to have a hold on you. Eventually, you begin to tell yourself, "I can't do anything about it." And if you say that long enough, all those dangerous, life-sucking patterns become *normal.*

When we're confronted with the truth about the habits in our lives that aren't leading us to satisfaction and fulfillment, in our frustration we learn to say, "Yeah, I know, but . . ."

"Yeah, I know it's really hurtful, but that's just how we talk to each other in our family."

"Yeah, I know I don't have a very good relationship with my kids, but putting in all the hours at work is just the way it is."

"Yeah, I know it's not completely honest, but that's just how we deal with people in our business."

"Yeah, I know I'm suffocating in debt, but that's just how I spend money."

We buy into the myth that the current condition of our lives is just the way it is—continuing to believe in Jesus but feeling frustrated with how things have turned out. It's sad how common this situation is.

Yet perhaps even more alarming and pervasive is the number of people who have simply become bored with it all.

Been There, Done That

Recently, at a neighborhood bistro, I had an eye-opening lunch with a friend I hadn't seen for a while. He's a former college football player, and though I'm not sure how he's managed to swing it, he still looks as if he could go out on the field and dominate, almost two decades after graduation. He's one of the most focused, driven people I've ever met, and he's been successful at just about everything he's ever tried, including his current gig as CEO of an online advertising company. He's married to a great woman, and they have three healthy, active kids. He gave his life to Christ in college, and he has been involved in some type of ministry ever since, usually as a leader.

Everything this guy touches turns to gold. And yet as soon as I saw him enter the restaurant, I sensed that all was not well. Although my friend wasn't exactly slouching, the way he carried himself gave the impression that he was living a much smaller life than his big, athletic frame would suggest.

"So, how have you been feeling lately?" I asked once the food had arrived at the table.

He was silent for a moment, moving his vegetables around with his fork while he thought about his reply. Finally, he shrugged and said, "Bored."

Given all that was going on in his life, and the success he has always enjoyed, I was surprised by his response.

"I always feel as if I'm in the midst of a swirl of energy," he said, "whether it's one of the initiatives I'm launching at work, the role I play as husband and father, or a ministry I'm heading up at church. What nobody knows is that most of the time I'm thinking, *Get me out of here.*"

Though his talent and hard work have delivered the goods

in terms of the kind of success that most of us seek, my friend said he has begun to face the fact that all his achievements and rewards haven't made his life any more satisfying. He isn't happy. Compared to where he thought he would be at this point in his journey of faith, his inner life seems pale and shrunken. And he has little excitement about the future. "I'm busy," he said, "but I'm bored so much of the time."

Fortunately, he has already begun to put his finger on what lies at the root of his disappointment. I know this because he said, "Here's what I can't figure out, Jason. How can I integrate Jesus into my everyday life?"

Jesus had become background music to his heavily scheduled life. My friend had gone on for weeks, then months, then years living his life—believing in Jesus the entire time—but never considering how his faith might affect every aspect of his life. He had put Jesus in the corner of the garage, pulling him out on Sundays and dusting him off for an occasional prayer during times of need. But once his faith became disconnected from his everyday life, it was just a matter of time before he became bored with just believing.

In my experience, boredom is the most common source of disappointment with our faith. It develops when we've lost sight of Jesus' promise that he can transform and revolutionize all aspects of our lives—the way we work, the way we parent, the way we love, the way we think, the way we spend our money, and the way we spend our time. Everything.

Too many of us have been lulled to sleep by the daily grind, never considering what it might look like to allow

Christ into all aspects of our lives—and we have grown bored with it all as a result.

What's Next?

When we're confronted with the disappointment that comes from bowing out, being beaten down, or growing bored with our faith, we're faced with a pressing question: What will we do next? Will we put the life that Jesus offers us up on a shelf, forever haunted by the thought of what might have been? Or is it possible to experience here and now the rich and satisfying life he promised?

Let's just confront this head-on. Let's own up to the secret we've carried around at times. Can we just acknowledge that we go through seasons when we're disappointed and disillusioned about the life of faith? And can we put a stake in the ground declaring that we will not let that stop us from experiencing and becoming all that God desires for us?

If this is where you are (or where someone you care about is), let me repeat: We don't have to settle for disappointment. A rich and satisfying life is not only possible; it's waiting for you to grab hold of it. Although the path toward that kind of life is not the easiest—it will require us to strike out in an unfamiliar direction over difficult terrain—it's the only path that will ever lead to *life* in the fullest sense.

I'll be honest—this issue is personal for me. I'm tired of seeing Christians settle for less. I'm tired of seeing Christians miss out on the life they've been promised because they have settled for just believing in Jesus and have never considered how Jesus might actually transform their everyday lives.

It's also personal for me because I've had one too many conversations with friends who see nothing compelling about following Jesus. All the Christians they know are beaten down, have bowed out, or have grown bored. Most people I know aren't looking at the lives of Christians and saying, "I gotta get me some of that!" In fact, for many, it's just the opposite.

Covering Up the Stink

My friend Travis stopped going to church years ago. One day when we were talking, I decided to get to the bottom of it.

"Why did you give up on church?" I asked.

"Let me tell you something that I don't think I've ever mentioned before," Travis said. "I can't smell anything. For instance, if you put an apple pie under my nose right now, I'd get nothing."

I've been in enough locker rooms over the years to know that Travis may have been given a gift without knowing it. But I knew that wasn't what he was saying, so I waited for him to connect the dots between his olfactory disability and his decision to abandon church.

"I remember going to a relative's house for Thanksgiving when I was a kid," he said. "When our family walked in, one of the first things my mom or dad would say was, 'It sure smells great in here!' Me, I didn't get even a whiff of the turkey and stuffing, much less the pumpkin pie. But everyone else seemed to agree about how great it all smelled. So I quickly learned that, if you want to make someone feel good, just say that whatever they're cooking smells great."

I nodded at Travis to keep the story going until it began to make sense.

"One time when I was in middle school," he continued, "I went to a friend's house when his mom was baking cookies. I couldn't smell the aroma, of course, but I remembered how happy it made people to get a compliment on the smell of their cooking. So I tried an experiment. I went up to my friend's mom and said, 'That smells great!' It was a total lie, but she got a big smile on her face and thanked me."

"So . . ." I began.

"So that's why I gave up on church," Travis said. "Every Sunday, I'd watch all the people walking around, saying to each other, 'It smells great in here!' But I knew some of the things that were going on in their lives outside of church. I knew some of their struggles. I knew how they treated their family members during the week. And I knew they couldn't smell a thing."

He went on to tell me about a case of child abuse that had come to light in his former church. Many people had known it was going on, but no one had acknowledged it, much less done anything to stop it. They were too busy walking around talking about how good everything smelled.

Travis saw how detached from reality people were at that church. He saw that their belief in Jesus had little bearing on the way they actually lived their lives. And it turned him off to Jesus altogether.

I couldn't say I blamed him. If that was what the Christian faith was all about, it left a lot to be desired.

Let's be honest: We can either face up to the fact that there are seasons when we are disappointed with our life of faith, or we can keep walking around talking about how great everything smells. But the cost of failing to deal with our disappointment is not merely that we will get stuck in dissatisfaction and fail to fulfill our potential. We may discourage *others* from pursuing Jesus as well.

So if you're living with an aching sense that there has to be more to faith than what you've been experiencing, I'm asking you—actually, I'm begging you—to *take action* to turn things around. Do it before the disappointment, frustration, or boredom gets any worse. You don't have to settle for a small life and a stale faith.

As a pastor, I've seen many people finally get to a place where their faith had grown so cold and stale that they coughed up the secret of their disappointment. But I've also had the privilege of hearing story after story of Christians who moved past just "believing in Jesus" and began to experience the fullness of life in relationship with him.

I've seen men and women who had relegated Jesus to a shelf in the closet establish new habits of faithfulness to him.

I've seen relationships that were tattered and torn be slowly stitched back together.

I've seen worship that had become merely routine get an injection of joy and passion.

I've seen friends who once pushed aside God's calling on

their lives take massive "leaps of obedience" into daring acts of faith.

I've seen the monotony of a nine-to-five job replaced by a sense of mission and purpose.

I've seen marketplace leaders reorient their perspective on profit.

I've seen men and women in the depths of depression find glimpses of life and hope.

I've seen the weight of addiction lifted off people's shoulders and carried away.

I don't believe that any of these people would ever dream of taking credit for the transformation they've experienced. They know that God was working in them through it all. Nor would they claim to have it all together in life. But when they look back at the past, they have the thrill of seeing that, slowly but surely, they have been moving forward toward the kind of life they dreamed of—the satisfying kind that Jesus promised.

They certainly haven't arrived yet, but they're moving. They're making progress.

And I can relate to that.

Proof of Life

If you were to take a look at a certain bookshelf in my office, you would find fourteen notebooks that tell the story of a man desperately searching for a rich and satisfying life in Jesus. They're the notebooks and sketch pads on which I've let my heart bleed over the years. Some of the writing is neat and orderly. Those are from the good seasons. Other sections, describing struggle, doubt, and failure, are scribbled and almost illegible, as if I were hoping that even God wouldn't be able to read my handwriting. Those pages tell the story of a heart in process.

Just the other day, I pulled them out again to flip through the pages. Here are a few stellar moments I scribbled down over the years:

"We have been fighting more ruthlessly than we have in the past."

"I lied today."

"I'm uninspired to love."

"I'm not long into my fast and I'm already thinking of how to cheat."

"My soul is drying up."

"I am tired of people and tired of giving. I'm especially tired of being tired."

And that's just the stuff I could bring myself to write down. But peppered throughout the notebooks are also these expressions of emerging life:

"God, whisper into my heart that I'm complete and I have what it takes."

"Today I've been reminded of grace."

"My heart feels so alive."

Two-steps-forward-one-step-back is the choreography that best describes how I've lived out my faith. That's why prayers that express an overwhelming sense of wonder over the experience of God's grace live right next door to prayers begging God for patience and mercy. My faith is not a picture of uninterrupted progress. It's not all up and to the right. *But I'm discovering that it's the only kind of faith worth having.* Because it's the kind of faith that actually transforms us. That works in us. That moves us forward.

Here's what else I observed while reading almost two decades' worth of my heart scribbled on paper: *I've changed.* Slowly, for sure. But I've changed. Or maybe I should say that I'm *changing.*

For the last couple of years, my wife, Jenny, and I have spent almost every Wednesday night with a group of friends who are committed to pursuing the life of Christ together. Andy leads our group, and he's one of my best friends.

A few months ago, Andy brought up a subject that I wasn't interested in talking about—mainly because it singled me out in front of the group. So I responded by defending myself.

Andy apparently picked up on my attitude, because he sat up straighter, moved to the edge of the couch, and looked me dead in the eye as he challenged me again.

I mirrored his posture, telling myself, *If he can sit up straight and move to the edge of the couch, so can I.*

The people in the group who valued harmony kept saying ridiculous things like, "Well, you both make really good points," but after a while, the chatter from the group and their growing unease faded into the background for me as I zeroed in on Andy's face. I tried to send him every signal I could think of—both verbal and nonverbal—that I was there to win and he was going to lose.

I dismissed his points.

He dismissed mine.

I spoke loudly.

He spoke louder.

This went on for several minutes, until I looked around and noticed that ten of our closest friends were staring at us in wide-eyed disbelief, wondering if we might actually throw down. It was a real possibility.

But instead of leaving each other with black eyes, Andy and I settled for silence and cold stares.

And thus concluded our Bible study for the evening.

I don't think we were even out of the driveway before Jenny said, "Hey, do you know you were kind of a jerk tonight?"

Yep. I knew. Which is why I didn't hesitate to call Andy the next morning to ask his forgiveness and offer him mine. And his gracious response helped mend what had been undone the night before.

I realize that calling a friend to repair a damaged relationship may not seem like a big deal. But for me, it was evidence that I'm growing and changing. Judging from my journal entries, if our argument had occurred even a few years earlier, it might have been days—if ever again—before I talked to

Andy. Although it still isn't easy for me to humble myself in order to ask for forgiveness or to forgive others, I see the need for it more clearly now, and I'm finding that I do it more readily than before.

If you were to read my journal entries in chronological order, you wouldn't find perfection, but progress: evidence that I really am different. This is the kind of forward motion we all can look back on with satisfaction if we're willing to take the right steps now.

It's like looking at photos of yourself from a previous decade. You may wonder who that person is—and who in the world let you leave the house looking like that. And even though you realize it's you in the photo, in another sense it's not you anymore at all. You aren't the same person.

There was a time when it took every ounce of willpower I had not to look at porn. If you had told me back then that there would come a day when such self-control would be easier for me, I'm not sure I would have believed you. All I knew in that season was the struggle. I hadn't yet built up the muscles of self-control. But day after day, as I decided to follow Jesus by honoring women in the way I thought about them, those muscles of self-control gradually strengthened. Early on, it seemed as if I was confronting this challenge every moment of every day. But it's no longer like that. The way I think about women today looks nothing like it did back then. And the same is true in other areas of my life.

The way I think about money has shifted.

I'm not as quick to lash out with my words when I'm offended.

I used to lie about everything. But as much as I'd like to occasionally spin the truth today, honesty tends to well up to the surface.

God only knows how much further I still have to go. I am fully aware of the struggles that still plague my heart—some subtle and some glaringly obvious. But I will not let the reality of how far I still have to go deny the truth that, by God's grace, I've changed and I'm still changing. I certainly don't want to stop now.

The story of my continued progress toward a life that is truly rich and rewarding will be told in journal entries I have yet to write. And I can't wait to find out what two-steps-forward-one-step-back stories those pages will tell.

I want that for you as well. I want you to move past discouragement, frustration, and boredom. I want you to experience life in all its fullness. I want you to blow the doors off small living and follow Jesus into a much bigger life. I want the ember that is still burning inside your heart to be fanned into flame. I want you to experience so much more than Jesus-on-a-shelf.

That's ultimately what this book is about. It's an exploration of the life that Jesus calls us to—a life that goes so much further than just *believing* in him, a life that pushes us into *living* for him. But as the title suggests, there's no easy Jesus here. Let me warn you right up front that a rich and satisfying life involves making some of the toughest choices you'll ever make in many key areas of your life and your relationships.

This book is not for the faint of heart. But if you grasp the biblical perspective I want to unpack for you, and if you choose to follow it, it will lead you to the greatest life possible.

You can start right now by deciding that your disappointment, frustration, and boredom will not define you. There's more to the life of faith than what you're currently experiencing.

And it's yours for the taking.

CHAPTER 2

GRIT

ONE NIGHT, when I was twenty years old, I locked myself in my bedroom.

"I'm not leaving this room," I said out loud to myself, "until I've decided once and for all whether I'm completely in or completely out on this Jesus thing."

It was 1998, and I was still living at home while attending the University of Louisville. I don't know how I could have been any more discouraged than I was in that season. I knew I couldn't go on the way I was going. I considered myself a Christian, yet nothing about my life remotely resembled Christ. I was suffocating under the lies I told. I was growing more isolated because of the hurt and pain I inflicted on the people around me. I lacked integrity in the literal sense of the word: My life was not integrated. There's no other way to be but miserable when you're living a divided life.

And I had been miserable for too long.

In the days before my bedroom lockdown, I had come face to face with the truth that I was a Christian by accident. It's easy enough to live this way when you grow up in a pastor's home. Faith was never something I really chose. I simply drifted into it as you would drift across a swimming pool on an inflatable raft if you closed your eyes. When I finally opened my eyes as a twenty-year-old college student, I realized I had somehow drifted into believing in Jesus.

That was why I locked myself in my room. I knew I believed in Jesus in the same way I believed in the power of love, or believed in my friends, or believed that the Cubs could win the World Series. None of those beliefs had any effect on the way I lived my life. I had no sense of participation in the life of Jesus. All that came from my accidental belief was a frustrating, unresolved conflict in my heart and mind. I became determined to deal with the tension that had been brewing under the surface of my life.

So when I walked to the end of the hallway in our suburban Louisville home, went into my bedroom, and shut the door, I decided I wasn't coming out until I had chosen either to follow Jesus with my whole heart or to be done with him once and for all.

Over the next two hours, I went back and forth in my

mind. I tried to imagine what my life would be like if I had no care or concern for what God might be asking of me.

I was drawn to the seeming freedom of that path.

But I also thought about the men and women I knew whose lives were completely oriented around Jesus. I was compelled by the joy, peace, kindness, and love that seemed to radiate from them. Their lives were what I wanted my life to look like one day.

If I was going to leave that bedroom having chosen Jesus, I knew it couldn't be a "dip your toes in the water" kind of decision. It had to be a "jump in the deep end even though you don't know how to swim" kind of thing. I would have to *own* my faith in Jesus—a faith I had consciously chosen, not just drifted into; a faith I was living out, not just playing at.

I would have to move past just *believing* in Jesus to actually begin *following* him.

Could I do that?

Did I want to?

All of these thoughts flooded my mind as I sat on my bed, elbows on knees, wrestling, praying, cussing, struggling, considering, and finally surrendering.

No Easy Jesus

On the night of the bedroom lockdown, my eyes were opened for the first time to the fact that, for years, I had settled for an "easy Jesus." This easy Jesus was a Jesus who didn't ask too much of me. His commands were more like suggestions—take 'em or leave 'em. Easy Jesus was a Jesus I could believe in without having to live any differently as a result. Apart from providing some nice principles to live by, this easy Jesus allowed me the space to continue my life the way I wanted. He gave me the promise of eternal life in heaven but conveniently left me alone in this life.

I think that many people who consider themselves Christians are in the same situation I was in. They believe in Jesus—Son of God, died on the cross, rose again—but haven't gone much beyond that. Sure, they participate in church (maybe); they read the Bible every now and then (maybe); and they share the always-helpful "praying for you" comments on Facebook. But if you were to take away those few obligatory demonstrations of faith, their lives would be no different than if they didn't know Jesus at all.

To be honest, we *love* an easy Jesus, because an easy Jesus covers us for eternity while giving us all the latitude we need to live our own lives.

But an easy Jesus isn't the *real* Jesus.

The truth is, we will never encounter the real Jesus until we go beyond merely *believing* in him and actually start *following* him. Yes, it's much harder to follow than to merely believe. But following is the only route to the rich and satisfying life we desire.

As I discovered in my own life, it's possible to drift into believing in Jesus simply by being born into a Christian home or being forced to go to church somewhere along the way. But while it may be possible to believe by accident, we will never follow Jesus by accident. And following has always been the point. Following takes deliberate *focus*, *intention*, and *action*.

As I read the New Testament, I can't escape the fact that it talks more about following Jesus than it does about believing in him. Jesus' first call to his disciples was "Follow me," and this is the same call he gives to all who believe in him.[1] Jesus said, "Anyone who wants to serve me must follow me."[2] No easy-Jesus excuses accepted.[3]

Don't get me wrong—the New Testament talks a lot about believing in Jesus. Yet even the phrase "believing in" conveyed more significance with the first-century audience that Jesus addressed than it does for us today. For them, the power behind the idea of "believing in" Jesus wasn't in the word *believing*; it was in the word *in*, which carries with it the idea of *movement*—of entering a building or walking into a new space.[4] So when the first followers of Jesus talked about believing *in* him, they weren't just talking about a cognitive affirmation that Jesus was the Son of God who lived and died and rose again. Instead, they were describing a life in which we actively participate in the ways of Jesus. Like stepping into a space in which we've never been before, believing *in* Jesus means entering into a completely new way of living and being.

Yes, we need to believe in order to have faith. But at some point our faith in Jesus must blossom into *faithfulness* to Jesus if we are interested in growing as *followers* of Jesus.

Putting Down Roots

The apostle Paul gives voice to this dynamic interplay between faith and following in his letter to the Colossians, where he writes, "Just as you accepted Christ Jesus as your Lord, you must continue to follow him."[5] Experiencing a growing life in Christ doesn't stop at the *acceptance of Jesus* (belief); we must also *continue to follow him.*

As followers of Jesus, we have a calling on our lives to wake up each and every day, embrace God's faithfulness all over again, and live faithfully in response to it. The invitation is to commit our lives to Jesus again and again. To develop the tenacity it takes to actively follow him, wherever he may lead. We *participate* in his life by making small choices to follow him, countless times over, knowing that in the end we will "reap a harvest of blessing" and of "everlasting life."[6]

So how do we do that?

Paul continues in his letter to the Colossians: "Let your roots grow down into [Jesus], and let your lives be built on him. Then your faith will grow strong in the truth you were taught, and you will overflow with thankfulness."[7] This is an important truth: We move forward in our relationship with Jesus not by trying harder on our own but by rooting ourselves more deeply in him. That's where the strength and growth and life come from.

When our roots go deep, we have strength and stability. We aren't swayed by the changing winds of the times. We aren't knocked down by the storms. We are able to draw from immeasurable resources, no matter how dry our present circumstances may seem. When we are deeply rooted in the life of Jesus, when our foundation is safe and secure in him, then we are ready to be *built up*. And even though we continue to be works in progress, it's the word *progress* that defines us. When we are rooted, we can grow. We have *life* and *vitality*.

The deeply rooted life is the kind of life we were made for. And our roots grow deeper as the result of waking up each day with a renewed commitment to continue following Jesus.

You can call this faithfulness.

You can call it obedience.

But I like to call it *grit*.

A Little Bit of Grit

I love the word *grit*. It's a word we can touch and feel.

When we describe someone as having grit, we're talking about *tenacity*, a fierce determination. It's that quality that keeps us moving forward even though the odds are stacked against us. When we have grit, we know where we want to go, and we know we're going to get there, come hell or high water.

In 2004, psychologist Angela Duckworth decided to study the qualities and traits that determine success in reaching predetermined goals. Her research—which included cadets at the US Military Academy at West Point, salespeople at a timeshare company, students in Chicago public schools, and soldiers in the Green Berets—found that the most necessary quality for success isn't IQ, personal connections, or natural talent. It's *grit*. Duckworth defines grit as "passion and perseverance for very long-term goals."[8]

Grit is different from talent, education, abilities, and opportunities. Grit is what you have left in the bottom of the cup when each of those other factors has been used up. We can buy an education, our genetics can give us an edge in certain skill sets, and we can train to develop our abilities; but grit is the universally available trait that moves us forward in reaching our goals, even when we've reached the limits of our knowledge and skill.

Grit is the combination of passion and persistence that becomes the driving force behind our pursuit of the life we desire. To describe someone as gritty means that they demonstrate qualities such as these:

- Courage
- Resilience
- Tenacity
- Relentlessness
- Toughness
- Resourcefulness
- Stamina

Now let me ask you a question. If you were going to describe other Christians you know, would these be the first words that came to mind?

Let's get more personal. Are these words that you would use to describe *your own* faith?

Can you imagine how your faith might look different if you could tap into the resources above?

If your experience as a Christian isn't adding up to a rich and satisfying life, it may not be because of a lack of faith; it may be an injection of grit that is needed most.

Waiting for Nothing

Recently, I met with a couple who had been married for twenty years. A few weeks before we sat down together, the husband had broken off a nine-month affair that he had successfully kept secret from his wife. But when the other woman informed him that she was pregnant and that the child might be his, he decided to finally tell his wife what he had done.

When we met, the husband explained that he was going to get DNA testing to find out whether he was the father. If he wasn't, he planned to stay with his wife and try to work things out. But if the child was his, he was going to leave his wife for the other woman.

We might as well have been on the set of an afternoon talk show, but the tears that were flowing made it clear there was nothing staged about this painful situation.

When I asked the two of them how they'd ended up in this spot, they both agreed that their marriage had been unhappy and contentious for many years.

"We've prayed over and over and over again that our marriage would turn around," the wife said. "We've waited and waited, but it never happened."

And that was the problem.

They had waited and done nothing.

I can't help but wonder how things might have been different if, after praying that God would heal their marriage, they both had done the most loving thing they could think of for the other person at that moment. And then again the next day, and the day after that. Perhaps after several months or years of putting aside their own needs in favor of the other spouse, and after countless acts of sacrifice and love, they may have found that there was a relationship worth saving there.

Instead, they waited for the marriage they desired to be handed to them. And it wasn't.

For them, it wasn't desire and good intentions that were missing. It was grit. It was the relentless tenacity to run after what they said they wanted most. But instead, they just waited.

As much as I wish I could tell you that I can't relate to that couple, the truth is that I can. My desires and good intentions have never been the problem.

I *want* to consistently lay down my own desires in favor of my wife . . .

I *want* to raise my kids in a way that gives them solid direction for their lives and sets the stage for a great relationship with them after they leave home . . .

I *want* to exercise self-control when I'm being drawn down a destructive road . . .

I *want* to be the kind of friend who serves others at the drop of a hat . . .

I *want* to honor people, not just in my actions but also in the way I think about them . . .

I *want* the life of Jesus . . .

But if I were completely honest with you, I'd have to say that sometimes I want all of this handed to me. My intentions are good, but good intentions alone will never lead us to the life we've been promised. As Eugene Peterson says, "We don't become whole persons by merely wanting to become whole, by consulting the right prophets, by reading the right book. Intentions must mature into commitments if we are to become persons with definition, with character, with substance."[9]

At some point, intentions must mature into commitments. Good intentions can get behind the wheel, but unless grit hits the gas, you're not moving anywhere. Transformation comes on the other side of doing the hard work of going after the life you've been promised with unyielding grit.

Earning and Effort

With all this talk about grit, maybe you're starting to wonder what ever happened to that other *g* word—*grace*. Isn't following Jesus all about God's undeserved favor?

The answer is yes—sort of. We are made right with God by 100 percent pure, unfiltered grace. A grace that tells us there is nothing we can do to make ourselves any more loved and accepted by God than we already are. But this book isn't about how we are made right with God. I'm talking about what happens *after* we've been made right with God through faith in Jesus Christ. I'm talking about how we grow. I'm talking about what it means to follow Jesus.

Coming home to God is easy because Jesus has already done all the heavy lifting on our behalf—and we can't add to that. But growing in Christ, being transformed into his likeness, becoming who we were made to be, stepping into rich and full lives—well, that takes some grit.

Dallas Willard, in his book *The Great Omission*, says, "Grace is opposed to *earning*, not to effort. In fact, nothing inspires and enhances effort like the experience of grace. . . . *Becoming Christ-like never occurs without intense and well-informed action on our part.*"[10]

Salvation is a pure, unadulterated gift—*absolute grace*.

And it is that same grace that compels us to get up, get in the game, and live differently in light of all we've been given—*absolute grit*.

When we try to earn God's acceptance, our morality becomes the point, and duty becomes our motivation. We relate to God out of fear because we don't want to upset the slave master. We work and strive, trying to earn what is already ours to begin with. But grace says that we can't earn any more of God's love, nor can we lose an ounce of it because of anything we've done or ever will do. It's grace. It's a gift. It's ours for the taking. Trust it and receive it.

Grace is always opposed to *earning*, but it's not opposed

to *effort*. In fact, grace makes demands. Grace calls out the best from us. Grace reorients everything we thought we knew about life. Grace confronts us in ways that may be uncomfortable.

God's grace is a fighting kind of grace. It pokes and prods and confronts and pushes us toward the path that leads to a rich and satisfying life. Grace will not let us settle for mediocrity and small living. It compels us to change.

It's tempting to think that because God is gracious and loving, he'll just let everything slide, never holding us accountable for making tough choices or following through on them. But this picture of God as a doting grandfather is flawed—not just because it misrepresents mercy, but also because it completely misunderstands love. God's love for us is far too relentless—far too gritty—to let us stay the way we are.

Heavy vs. Hard

In Matthew 11:28-30, Jesus makes a fascinating statement to anyone willing to follow him:

> Come to me, all of you who are weary and carry heavy burdens, and I will give you rest. Take my yoke upon you. Let me teach you, because I am humble and gentle at heart, and you will find rest for your souls. For my yoke is easy to bear, and the burden I give you is light.[11]

Following Jesus isn't burdensome. It isn't a heavy load. His yoke is light and easy to bear because *he* bears the weight of it. The hoops we think we need to jump through in order to gain God's favor have crumbled under an earthquake of grace.

We can rest.

But here's the catch. The kind of rest that Jesus describes here is not a rest that comes from sitting back and doing nothing. It's the kind of rest and peace that come from knowing that the life we're pursuing is the only one that truly matters.

This is why, right in the middle of these promises from Jesus, we find a challenging invitation that we can't afford to gloss over: "Let me teach you . . ."

In our willingness to open ourselves to everything Jesus wants to teach us and show us, we may need to bend and conform our will to his. That's the hard part, and not everyone is willing to do it. In fact, there was a time when some people who were following Jesus responded to his instruction by saying, "This is a hard teaching. Who can accept it?"[12] And "from this time many of his disciples turned back and no longer followed him."[13]

Following Jesus will never be a heavy burden, but it may be hard at times. Jesus holds both these truths in the same hand.

His intense love for us won't have it any other way. It's his love that drives him to pursue us and push us back toward the paths that lead to life. His love and grace compel us to work and to change.

And along the way, he gives us everything we need to see it through.

Our *Parakletos*

My wife, Jenny, has run multiple marathons and half-marathons, but there was nothing quite like the thrill of her very first race.

Early that morning, Jenny made her way out of the house and drove to the starting line. Later that morning, the kids and I took up our stations at mile marker 9, joining an enthusiastic crowd there to cheer on the runners. We were decked out in our "Run, Jenny, Run" T-shirts, and we were ready to wave our homemade signs as soon as Jenny came into view.

While we waited, we were surrounded by hordes of people yelling encouragement to the runners as they came by.

"You can do it!"

"Keep going!"

"Not much farther!"

"You've got this!"

Something powerful happened when those men and women, in dogged pursuit of their predetermined goals, were surrounded by the voices of others reminding them that they had what it took to keep going. You could see a physical change in some of them. Something in them was lifted. They found new energy.

It's interesting to me that when Jesus describes the Holy Spirit, he uses the word *Advocate*, which comes from the Greek word *parakletos*, meaning "one called alongside." Jesus is describing an intimate picture of the Holy Spirit walking alongside us, calling out to us.

Think about what those people lining the road that day were really doing. They were playing the role of *parakletos*. They were coming alongside those who were running the race, and they were speaking words of life into them. Encouraging them. Lifting them up. Reminding them that they had trained for this and that everything would be okay.

In John 14, Jesus promises that the Holy Spirit would live in us as our Parakletos—calling out to us, reminding us of who we are, leading us, guiding us, empowering us, and helping us. In short, the Holy Spirit is God's provision for us when it feels like the grit we need to keep following Jesus has reached its limits.

In his letter to the Philippians, the apostle Paul describes the dynamic relationship of grace and grit working in unison: "Work hard to show the results of your salvation, obeying God with deep reverence and fear. For God is working in you, giving you the desire and the power to do what pleases him."[14]

Again we see the importance of not merely believing in Jesus but of following him as well. We work hard to show the results of our salvation, obeying God with gritty faithfulness. And at the same time, God is working in us.

It's right in the middle of this intersection between grit and grace that Paul throws out two incredibly important words: *desire* and *power*.

Like grit and grace, desire and power work together.

Desire without power would be pointless. We can have all the desire in the world to live in ways that please God, but without the power to actually do it, we'd just be spinning our wheels while growing frustrated. Likewise, we could have all the power we need to live lives of faithfulness to God, but with no desire to live that way, the power would be wasted. But what Paul is saying is that we have been given both the desire and the power to live the life that God has for us.

The Spirit of God lives in us, strengthening us and empowering us to say no to the paths that will not lead to life and yes to those that do. The Spirit reminds us again and again of the grace we've been given, supplying us with all the grit we need to move forward.

The Holy Spirit stands on the side of the road speaking into us what we need to hear when we need to hear it: "You've got this. I know it's tough. I know you have to pull from deep reserves of grit, but I have given you all the desire and power you need to keep going. Don't stop! Keep following!"

The Spirit reminds us that in the end, rejecting an easy Jesus and pursuing the real Jesus is the only race worth running. It's the only path that can lead us to fullness of life.

If we're going to respond to the Spirit's voice calling out to us, it will mean *choosing* to follow Jesus—again and again and again.

Between Wednesday and Friday

When I finally emerged from my bedroom that November night in 1998, I was changed. I knew it. I had committed to something—following Jesus—that I hadn't done before. And just as surely as I'm sitting here now writing these words, I knew then that a new and better life lay before me.

That was on a Wednesday.

On Friday I went to a strip club with some friends.

Looking back, I'm not sure why I went. I thought about saying no, but somehow I never worked up the nerve. For one of the first times in my life, I sensed the Holy Spirit whispering warnings in my ear. But my friends and I had already agreed to go, my commitment to Jesus hadn't caught up to my hormones yet, and frankly I got scared thinking about how I would explain backing out to my friends. So I did the easy thing and went.

It wasn't my first time going to the club with my friends, but this time was different. With fresh eyes and a renewed conscience, I saw each of the women as someone's sister, daughter, wife, or girlfriend. I looked at myself, my friends, and the other men at the club, and I sensed the selfishness of it all. Beyond that, I felt guilt. Not a shaming, condemning kind of guilt, but the kind of guilt that comes from knowing the sort of life that's possible and yet choosing not to choose it. I knew that God desired so much more for me and for every last person at the club that night, yet I had chosen an obvious detour from the path that would lead me there.

The next day, I woke up feeling something else: *frustration*. But I wasn't frustrated with myself for choosing to go to the strip club. I know it sounds ridiculous, but I was frustrated with Jesus for not stopping me!

Had he forgotten about that Wednesday night encounter

we'd had? I thought he was supposed to make temptation a distant memory and help me avoid sin. I thought he was supposed to give me victory over my struggles. I thought he would magically put up roadblocks to all the destructive paths I could take. I thought the only things I would want to do from that point on would be to listen to worship music and read the Bible.

I thought the decision I'd made that Wednesday to follow Jesus was all I needed to experience a relationship with him. I didn't know I'd have to choose to follow him again on Friday and every day thereafter—that I'd have to "continue following." I didn't know that the grace that had flooded my heart would now make demands on my life.

Anytime you try walking for the first time, those initial steps are a bit wobbly. I've already admitted to you that I still have some wobble in me. And so do you. But let's wake up tomorrow and choose to stand up and walk again—toward the real Jesus and away from the easy Jesus.

What matters more than anything else is that we keep moving forward—one step at a time.

Take the Next Step

A few years back, when I was in South Carolina on vacation with my family, I decided one day to go out for a run. As much as I would love to tell you that I'm as good a runner as my wife is, the Holy Spirit is on the side of the road, calling out to me right now that lying to you won't lead me to a rich and satisfying life. The truth is, Jenny's a runner and I'm a jogger. On this occasion, however, I decided to push myself harder than I'd ever pushed myself before. I decided on the number of miles I wanted to cover, and it was the farthest I had ever run. Still, I was determined to complete the course no matter what.

I came up with an easy plan to gauge my distance. Near the place where we were staying, there was a long, straight road running parallel to the beach. It was lined on both sides with hotels and condos. Once I hit the halfway point, a spot marked by a water tower, I would simply turn around and run the same road back.

I put my earbuds in, set my eyes on that water tower, and started moving. It wasn't long before I was sweating under the oppressive South Carolina sun. Worse than that, a constant wind was blowing in my face as I traveled down the road. This was not a refreshing breeze; it was more like a giant hairdryer pointed straight at me. But I kept running.

Finally, when I looked up ahead, I could see that the water tower marking my turnaround point was close. Only then did it begin to sink in that once I reached the water tower, I was only halfway done with my run. I still had the entire return trip ahead of me.

Instantly, I felt defeated. I was tired and struggling. It was all I could do to convince myself to keep putting one foot in front of the other, each step now representing a monumental accomplishment of focus and willpower.

As I ran, I began repeating a phrase rhythmically in my head.

Just take the next step.
Just take the next step.
Just take the next step.

After doing that more times than I could count, I finally arrived at the water tower and turned my worn-out body around to start heading back.

As I made the turn, I noticed something. Although it was still just as hot outside, and I still had a long way to go before I was home, the wind was now at my back, gently pushing me in the right direction.

I find it interesting that the Holy Spirit is often described in the Bible as a wind. (Perhaps the writers were also runners?) Like a steady breeze, the Holy Spirit pushes us along as we put one foot in front of the other in life. He isn't overbearing; he doesn't do all the work for us; but he partners with us to get us home. His grace, our grit.

To be honest, the return leg of my run that day in South Carolina was still difficult. But now I had the wind at my back. I was able to do what I had to do in order to go where I wanted to go—I took the next step.

That's how transformation and growth always happen in life. That's how the gap between who we are right now and who God calls us to be is gradually closed—one gritty step at a time.

When we reject the easy Jesus in search of the real Jesus, we take a step. When we convert our desire and intention into *commitment*, we take a step. Day in and day out, with each seemingly small decision to align our lives with the way of Jesus, we take a step. And before we know it, with a little bit of grit and the Wind at our backs, we find that we've covered some ground. We've moved forward in running after the rich and satisfying life that we desire.

My greatest hope is to encourage you to reject the false promises of the easy-Jesus approach. Believe me, you want the real Jesus, even when following him can be difficult. Besides, you have a lot more grit than you realize. You just need to apply it to your faith in Jesus and get on with the business of actively following him.

In the chapters ahead, I want to show you how to combine grit and grace in seven key areas of life where Jesus invites us to make the toughest choices. I promise it will transform the way you see relationships with the people you love and those whom you now consider enemies. It will change your perspective on caring for the people around you who are in need. It will reorient your relationship to money and possessions. It will require courage to face up to things that you may have been avoiding.

Do you want the fullness of life that Jesus offers?

If so, grit and grace will take you there.

CHAPTER 3

ABSORBING THE DEBT

ONE OF THE BEST THINGS about being a pastor is getting to hear people's stories. It's also one of the worst parts of the job. I can't tell you how many stories I've heard that put on display some of the darkest ways that people treat each other.

Stories of husbands lying about where they've been and whom they've been with.

Stories of wives walking out on their families.

Stories of being cheated on, used, abused, exploited, neglected, ignored, stolen from, and dumped on.

I'm sure you have stories of your own. It probably wouldn't take long for you to make a list of the ways you've been offended, wounded, or mistreated by others. The problem might be in knowing where to stop.

Whenever we've been wronged, one incredibly tough choice will always confront us: Will we "forgive those who sin against us"?[1]

The easy choice is to hold on to the ways in which we've been wronged, replaying the offenses over and over again in our minds, looking to even the scales whenever we get a chance. But there's nothing that requires more grit than offering forgiveness when we've been wronged—because by all appearances, forgiveness only adds one injustice to another. Forgiving someone who has wronged us is the toughest of choices, because everything in us resists giving up our right to get back and get even.

When we contemplate forgiveness, our hearts scream out, *We've been treated in ways we didn't deserve. Why should we let the other person off the hook? He or she should be doing something to make it right with us!*

Forgiveness seems so unfair.

That's because it is.

Forgiveness doesn't use the same scales that justice does.

Choosing to forgive means that we absorb the debt we are owed by the person who wronged us. That's painful. That's difficult. But let's be honest: When we've been wronged, our choice is really between two difficult and painful options. We can choose the pain of absorbing the debt and releasing the person who wronged us, or we can choose the pain that comes with holding on to the offense.

But here's the difference: The pain that comes with forgiveness is temporary, like the pain of setting a broken bone.

It may hurt *a lot* at the moment—let's not minimize it—but once it's done, we know that the injury will heal in time and the pain will fade as forgiveness frees us from the ongoing agony of bitterness.

That's why I want to explore forgiveness as the first tough choice for anyone interested in following the real Jesus instead of an easy Jesus—because so many people get stuck there. They waste their lives, steeped in resentment and weighed down by grudges, and yet they haven't exercised the grit necessary to deal with their pain in the way that Jesus invites us to: *Forgive as you have been forgiven.*[2]

Forgiveness is the only path that will ultimately lead you to freedom from the mental, emotional, and spiritual chains that wrap themselves around an offended heart. Like trying to run a race while dragging heavy weights behind you, you'll never be able to move freely toward the life you want while hanging on to bitterness and resentment.

That's no way to live.

And forgiveness is the only way forward.

Ordinary Enemies

If you grew up in the church or have spent time reading the Bible, odds are that you've heard a lot about forgiveness. But have you ever considered what the word actually means?

When Jesus explored the topic of forgiveness, he talked about it in ways that moved it from sentimentality into concrete action. Consider his words: "To you who are willing to listen, I say, love your enemies! Do good to those who hate you. Bless those who curse you. Pray for those who hurt you."[3]

Anytime Jesus starts a teaching by saying, "To you who are willing to listen," you can assume that whatever he's about to say next will be confrontational in the most life-giving way. In this brief passage from the Gospel of Luke, there are four commands that are packed with potential to stir us up. It's worth taking a closer look in order to understand the powder keg that Jesus ignites here.

"Love . . ."

We have all sorts of ideas about what it means to love, and most of them revolve around *feelings*. The word translated as *love* in this passage, however, is light-years away from sentimentality. For Jesus, love is an action-oriented, sacrificial, work-up-a-sweat commitment to do what's right for another person. This kind of love proves itself in a willingness to give until it hurts.

"Do good . . ."

The word translated as *good* in this passage is tied to the Greek word *kalos*, which carries with it the idea of pursuing what is "right and beautiful." So when Jesus talks about "doing good," he is describing a kind of life in which we make right what is wrong. It's a life centered on bringing beauty to what has been marred and broken.

"Bless . . ."

The idea of blessing someone is pretty straightforward. It's a translation of the Greek word *eulogeo*, which literally means "to speak good words" about someone.

"Pray for . . ."

In the New Testament, the word *pray* is tied to the idea of well-wishing. In the context of this passage, when Jesus tells us to pray he is talking about our *desiring the best* for someone. We desire God's favor for the people we pray for, wanting them to flourish.

My guess is that we all would agree that *loving, doing good, blessing,* and *praying* are all good ways to live. The tension comes from who Jesus says should be the recipients of these actions.

- Love . . . *your enemies.*
- Do good . . . *to those who hate you.*
- Bless . . . *those who curse you.*
- Pray for . . . *those who hurt you.*

So ask yourself, *Who is my enemy?*

We tend to associate a word like *enemy* with villains on a grand scale. This allows us to detach ourselves a bit from what Jesus requires of us. After all, most of us aren't fighting any true villains. But when Jesus refers to our enemies, he's talking about something much more common and ordinary. As he's using the term here, an enemy is anyone who has taken something from you. This could be anything from taking your parking spot at the mall during the holidays to taking your innocence. It could be taking your time and wasting it or taking advantage of your trust. It might be taking a shot at your character or taking a shot at your spouse.

So I'll ask again: Who is your enemy?

Who has wronged you? Who has wounded you?

Who has hated you? Who has made it a point to be cruel to you? Who has embarrassed you?

Who has mocked you? Who has gossiped about you? Who has trashed your reputation?

Who has used you? Who has broken your trust? Who in your life always takes and never gives?

Okay, now that you finally have names and faces in mind, consider how deeply challenging Jesus' words are.

Love them with the kind of love that makes sacrifices.

Bring beauty to their lives, setting right what was wrong.

Speak good words about them.

When you talk to God about them, ask him to make their lives flourish.

You can see now why Jesus started by saying that this is for "you who are willing to listen." There's nothing easy about forgiveness.

Even grace takes grit.

The Cycle of Recycled Revenge

When I first met Julia, she was an angry twelve-year-old, and for good reason. Do you remember being twelve? That age can be hard enough without having to deal with an addiction in the home.

Julia's dad was an alcoholic, and because of him Julia had already endured years of broken promises, fumbled attempts at sobriety, fights, arrests, and countless regrets.

Julia told me one day that she had written her dad a stack of letters telling him how she felt.

I said, "That's great! What did you say to him?"

"I told him how much I hate him."

"Oh. Then I take back what I said about this being a great thing."

"I told him that it's only a matter of time before I move out," Julia continued, "and then he'll never see my face again. I told him he will never walk me down the aisle at my wedding, and he will never be involved in my life once I'm an adult. I want him to know he has given up all that because of his choices."

Hurt is the fertile ground in which resentment puts down roots. When Julia loaded her pen with resentment and started writing, with each pain-filled word she slipped further toward becoming just like the person she had grown to hate. Out of her own hurt, she had become someone who wanted to hurt in return.

I love how Coldplay puts it in one of their songs:

I don't want a cycle of recycled revenge.
I don't want to follow death and all of his friends.[4]

That's where resentment leads us. We keep recycling in our minds all the events, words, and actions that have caused us pain. We keep scheming and plotting how we'll get back at those who have wounded us. And before long, it leads to a kind of death inside of us.

When we refuse to let go of revenge, we end up living out the very things that caused us pain in the first place. We fill our letters with the very words that have crushed us. We abandon others because we won't let go of being abandoned. We hate those who hated us, reject those who rejected us, and hurt those who hurt us. Maybe you are stuck right now in a cycle of recycled revenge, and it's because you refuse to consider even the possibility of forgiving those who have wronged you.

But as impossible as it may seem, forgiveness is a path we can choose, because our gritty resolve is rooted not just in our human will but also in the very nature of our merciful God.

Joining God

There is a sacred connection between how we relate to other people and how we relate to God. That's why Jesus says, "Forgive others, and you will be forgiven."[5] In other words, we can't be wrong with others and right with God. We tend to love the idea that God forgives us, even when we were his enemies,[6] yet we resist forgiving our own enemies. But Jesus essentially says, "You can't have it both ways."[7]

Why? It's not because God wants to make our lives even harder than they are but because forgiveness is intricately woven into the fabric of the life he wants us to have. Any hope we have for stepping into the life that Jesus promises is purely the result of God's decision to relentlessly pour out forgiveness on us.

Throughout the Bible, God is described as a limitless pool of mercy, forgiveness, and grace. Over and over again, we find descriptions of God like this one in Psalms:

> The LORD is compassionate and merciful,
>   slow to get angry and filled with unfailing love.
> He will not constantly accuse us,
>   nor remain angry forever.
> He does not punish us for all our sins;
>   he does not deal harshly with us, as we deserve.
> For his unfailing love toward those who fear him
>   is as great as the height of the heavens above the
>   earth.
> He has removed our sins as far from us
>   as the east is from the west.[8]

God's merciful and compassionate character is put on full display when he removes our sins from us. He looks at us and says, "You may have *done* that wrong, but you aren't *defined* by that wrong."

Do you believe that? Do you believe it in the deepest part of your being? Have you allowed the inexhaustible love and forgiveness of God to wash over you so completely that there isn't a spot on you that isn't drenched with grace?

When Jesus says that we will be forgiven only if we choose to forgive, he is ultimately confronting us about the fundamental way in which we view God. On the surface, he appears to say that if we choose not to forgive others, then God will choose not to forgive us. But God can't be bought. His forgiveness is free and unlimited. Rather, Jesus is saying that when we refuse to forgive others, it's a sign that we've forgotten the plot of the story we're in. We've lost sight of the essential character of God. We've forgotten our own brokenness and dependence on him. Ultimately, if we refuse to forgive others, we won't experience God's forgiveness—not because he will withhold it but because we won't think we need it.

Loving those who have offended us, speaking well of those who have hurt us, and doing good to those who have wronged us have little to do with Jesus wanting his followers to be nice people. Jesus isn't giving his followers more commands; he's giving us a glimpse of a life lived in tune with God's character. Forgiveness and grace are rooted in the reality of who God is. When we forgive as we have been forgiven, our character is reshaped by his. These ways of being are visible expressions of God's character and the work that he's doing in us and in the world.

This is why Jesus says, "Be merciful, just as your Father is merciful."[9] This might sound like a lofty ideal that is impossible to actually live up to. But the key to that sentence is the word *as*, which points to the ongoing reality that God is *already* at work in the world, unleashing compassion, mercy, grace, and forgiveness on everyone who will receive it—including you and me. And when we do the difficult work of forgiving, loving, and praying for our enemies, we *join* God in the redemptive work he is already up to in the world.

When we make the hard choice to offer forgiveness to someone who doesn't deserve it, we put the character of God on full display for all to see. We announce with our lives, "This is the God who carries away our sins and doesn't hold them against us, so I will not hold your sin against you."

I realize that you may think I have to talk about forgiveness in these ways because I'm a pastor. But I don't. Forgiveness isn't a point of theology to me. It isn't a mere ideal. I'm not interested in pursuing pipe dreams any more than you are. I'm interested in discovering how the world really works and getting in tune with it. I'm interested in a *practical* faith, in what actually works in leading us toward the rich and satisfying life that Jesus promised. If forgiving those who have wronged us doesn't move us forward, I don't want any part of it, no matter how pure and beautiful the idea may sound.

Forgiving those who have wronged us is far too hard and takes way too much grit to talk about casually. It is painful and awkward.

I know this all too well.

What No One Should Go Through

When I was nine years old, my family moved from Georgia to North Carolina, where my father was going to take over the pastorate of a church. We moved in October, and in January a blizzard hit the region. It was the first snow I'd ever seen, and it closed school for a week. A week! This in itself convinced me that we were not in North Carolina—we were in heaven.

But it wouldn't be long before I discovered just how far from heaven we really were.

My family was always welcoming to everyone. We got involved in people's lives, invited them into our home, and allowed them to share in our lives, as well. So when we moved to North Carolina and met Mike, a middle-aged member of our church who had no wife or kids, it seemed natural to open our home to him and love him as if he were a part of our family. We had Mike over for Sunday lunch. He took part in family birthday parties. He helped fix things at the house. Gradually, he spent more and more time with us.

Mike took a particular liking to me. We talked about things I was interested in, and he started inviting me over to his townhome on Sunday afternoons so we could play video games and build model space shuttles together.

I found out quickly that Mike wanted more from me than just hanging out. For almost five years, he sexually abused me.

I hated Sundays.

I'm not sure that anyone who hasn't been through an experience like this can understand how trapped I felt. I was ashamed, convinced it was all my fault. Mike told me that if the situation ever got out in the open, our church would dissolve. Even worse, he told me repeatedly that he would kill himself if anyone found out. For five years I lived every day feeling as if I had the well-being of an entire church and a man's life in my hands.

So I kept quiet, slowly withering away on the inside.

One day, when I was fourteen, both my parents came to pick me up from school. This was unusual because it was typically just my dad who picked me up, so I wondered what was going on. Then, instead of driving home, my dad took a right turn out of the school and drove to a nearby parking lot. He parked in a remote corner of the lot and turned off the engine.

Complete silence. I watched my dad reach down deep into his heart to find the words to say to his wounded son.

Finally, in a hollowed-out voice, my dad said, "Jason, we know everything that's happened. And it's going to be okay."

That morning, my parents had found a letter I had written to Mike, telling him that I never wanted to see him again because of what he had done.

At that moment, five years' worth of shame, pain, and confusion came flooding over me.

We went straight to the police and prepared ourselves for whatever it would take to see justice run its course with Mike. But we couldn't anticipate how much hurt was still to come.

Because Mike was a well-connected, longtime member of the church, our accusations against him set off a whirlwind of reaction in the congregation. Friends turned their backs on us. Men and women I had looked up to and respected wrote me letters telling me it was my fault. Other families isolated themselves from us, not wanting to take sides.

At Mike's trial, half a dozen people from our church, including some members of my dad's leadership team, took the stand to testify as character witnesses for Mike. They asked the judge to pardon him.

In the end, the judge saw through everything that was said, and justice was served as she sentenced Mike to twenty years in prison. But the situation at the church would never be the same.

Sometimes you just need to hit the "reset" button in life. Which is exactly what we did. We packed up and moved to Kentucky, where our bruised and battered hearts began to heal. The people in our new church walked patiently beside us as we recovered from our wounds.

Over time, I began to wrestle with what it might mean to forgive Mike. Some days, it was easy to think about. Other days, it seemed impossible. I knew it was possible that Mike himself had been abused as a child, and there were days when I felt mercy well up inside me, desiring him to be delivered from his own pain. But then there were days when I wished he were dead. Back and forth I went between those two competing impulses.

Along the way, I've discovered that the door of forgiveness doesn't necessarily shut behind you once you've chosen to walk through it. You can always walk back out. And even if you walk back out, the door stays open. Eventually, the more you choose to forgive, the easier it becomes to walk through the door and not look back.

In time, I felt that I had forgiven Mike as well as I was

able and had put the whole painful experience behind me. I imagined those five years like a chapter in my life story that I'd rather not read about ever again. I figured I'd just turn the page and move on to the next chapter.

I wish it had been that simple.

Forgive and Never Forget

The spring of 2002 was an eventful season in my life. Jenny and I were in our first year of marriage, I was graduating from college, and we were preparing to move to Pennsylvania for my first full-time ministry role.

Also that spring, I received a letter from the North Carolina Department of Corrections informing me that Mike had been granted parole and would be released in May. I didn't think much about it at the time, but apparently the news continued to lurk in the background of my mind.

On the day before my college graduation ceremony in May, we had a rehearsal—one of those rare times in life when grown men and women are reminded how to stand in a straight line, listen for their names to be called, and walk across a stage from one side to the other. In addition to all the graduates, a smattering of parents and other family members also were seated in the auditorium.

As the coordinator for the ceremony ran through the order of ceremony, I glanced out into the small crowd—and froze.

I saw Mike.

I was jarred out of my frozen state by some kind of primal instinct that took over . . . and I ran to the bathroom. Feeling numb, I splashed water on my face while saying over and over in my mind, *What am I going to do? What am I going to do?*

For the next five minutes or so, I stared blankly at myself in the mirror, unable to move. Then something happened. With a newfound resolve, I snapped out of my daze and said out loud to myself, "What am I doing here, trapped in the bathroom? Mike doesn't have any power over me. He's not in control anymore."

As I walked back in to the auditorium, I took a deep breath and strode directly over to Mike, glaring right into his eyes. But when I got a few feet away from him, I paused.

It wasn't him.

With as much dignity as I could summon, I quickly moved on, no doubt leaving the poor man I'd been glaring at wondering what in the world had just happened.

"Forgive and forget" is about as unhelpful a piece of advice as you can give to anyone who's ever been wronged. When we've been badly hurt, we *can't* forget. Nor *should* we in many cases.

But that doesn't mean we can't forgive.

Like a scratched CD that gets stuck on a single note, I had not allowed Mike to move on from the one role he had played in my life. In my mind, the CD kept skipping at the same point: *abuser, abuser, abuser.* Here's the thing: My unwillingness to let him move on from that single note wasn't keeping *him* stuck. It was keeping *me* stuck. I was the one who was running to the bathroom. By not allowing Mike to move beyond that one note, I hadn't been able to move on either.

You may never have been on the receiving end of sexual abuse or some other tragic form of injustice. I hope you haven't. But there will be countless times in your life—maybe even today—when you will be wronged in some small way. Someone will waste your time. Someone will disrespect you. Someone will ignore you. Someone will cut you off. Forgiveness in those day-to-day moments is just as critical as it is in the big moments.

Here's why. Our willingness to forgive others for big offenses is directly proportional to our willingness to forgive small offenses. In other words, if we grow skilled at practicing ongoing forgiveness when the stakes are relatively small, we strengthen our ability to forgive when the big moments arrive. But if we refuse to forgive even small offenses, we don't stand a chance if we're ever on the receiving end of a big one.

The Other Victory

Theologian Miroslav Volf makes the point that evil needs two victories in order to be triumphant. "The first victory happens when an evil deed is perpetrated; the second victory, when evil is returned" as revenge.[10]

Remember, our enemies are those who have taken

something from us. Whenever something is taken from us—be it our trust, our innocence, or anything else—there is always a debt to be paid. Either the other person pays or we pay.

Forgiveness means we swallow up the wrong that was done to us. It requires that we absorb the pain instead of inflicting more of it. When we choose to forgive wrongs, we prevent them from going any further. That's why forgiveness always involves a bit of suffering but also why there is no more powerful force in overcoming evil.

It may also explain why we are attracted to the *idea* of forgiveness while at the same time wanting nothing to do with having to offer it. We know that, in the short term at least, it means *absorbing* pain rather than inflicting it. We feel the cost of forgiveness in our bones.

Especially when we've been the victims of injustice, absorbing the debt feels like the most counterintuitive thing we could do. It's almost foolish to even contemplate. That's why we will never *accidentally* forgive someone. We will never just happen to pray for our enemies or speak well of those who have wounded us. We won't inadvertently love the person who's taken something from us. We can only do it deliberately, with determination and grit.

The entire Christian story revolves around the plotline of forgiveness. It is centered on a bloodied and bruised Savior, who took all evil and sin committed against him and absorbed it, forgave it, washed it away. He paid for what was taken from him. And that's why the Cross changes things.

The way of the Cross means that we now agree with God that a new day and hope for tomorrow is possible because nobody's sin is beyond redemption.

One last time, think about the name and face of the "ordinary enemy" who came to your mind at the beginning of this chapter. Think about the wrongs committed against you that are still rattling around inside your brain because you have not yet released them. If you will choose to follow Jesus by engaging in the difficult work of forgiveness, you will join with a God who's already at work in the world bringing restoration and wholeness. By choosing to forgive, you will boldly proclaim to the world—and to those who have wronged you—that evil, sin, injustice, and pain will not have the final word here.

You will be free.

Who Gives This Woman?

I always wondered how Julia's story would play out after she told me about the letters she had written to her dad. Several of us at the church spent a lot of time trying to help her work through her anger and bitterness. But throughout her teen years, Julia sank deeper into resentment toward her father and all the things he had done.

A few years passed, and after Julia left home she began to realize that holding on to the pain her dad had caused her—holding it over him, demanding that he pay for what he had taken from her—had actually kept her stuck on one note. Gradually, she began the painful process of forgiveness, choosing to absorb the debt she was owed and releasing her father from having to pay for the offenses he had handed her. It was tremendously difficult—an epic act of the will—but she also knew that the endless cycle of recycling revenge was no way to live.

Her father, for his part, began to get his addiction under control and to live a somewhat more responsible life.

So what effect has Julia's decision to grit her teeth and choose forgiveness had on their relationship?

I don't know all the ins and outs of their family dynamic today. But what I do know is this: Recently, I stood at the front of a small chapel where Julia and her fiancé had come to get married. As the bridesmaids completed their processional, I watched as the doors at the back of the chapel swung open to reveal a radiant bride.

And standing right next to Julia was her father, ready to walk her down the aisle.

CHAPTER 4

SKIN IN THE GAME

A FEW YEARS AGO, I was driving home at the end of a rainy spring day. My first clue that something was wrong came when I looked down the glossy road and noticed that the drivers ahead of me were hitting their brakes.

Approaching the source of the slowdown, I saw a conversion van turned around in the middle of the road and a small white car with severe damage to the back end resting in a nearby field. The accident had evidently happened only moments before, and it looked like a bad one.

A man ran over to the car in the field, and as he peered into the back of it, his face went pale. I knew that whatever he was seeing wasn't something I wanted to see.

By this point, several people had gathered around the accident scene and were yelling instructions for those of us still in our cars to move along. As I headed down the road toward home, fire trucks and ambulances passed me on their way to the scene I had just left.

The next day, my heart sank when I read in the paper that two teenagers had died in the back seat of that small white car.

A few days later, as I was traveling home again and approaching the spot where the accident had happened, I noticed a dozen or so cars parked on the side of the road. Just off the pavement, a large group of people were crying and hugging. These had to be friends and family of the kids who had been killed.

This simple prayer erupted from my heart: "God, please comfort them."

I could still see the mourners in my rearview mirror when I sensed that God was speaking into my heart: "Of course I want to comfort them. So go do it. Go comfort them."

I turned my car around and drove back toward the group. But the closer I got, the more I tried to rationalize my way out of following through on God's clear leading.

I don't even know these people.

Who am I to intrude on their grieving?

How are they going to respond if I just come walking up to them?

What would I even say?

So I turned around again to go home, hoping I could just

ignore everything when I passed by this time. But I couldn't. I drove by the accident scene two more times, still waffling between what I knew God was leading me to do and my unwillingness to actually do it. Finally, I was able to ignore my inner objections just long enough to pull over to the side of the road.

One woman in the group was undoubtedly the mother of one of the accident victims—she was about the right age, and her overwhelming grief was obvious. Setting aside the last of my reservations, I walked up to her, put my arms around her, drawing her head against my chest, and whispered, "I am so sorry for your loss." I don't think I'll ever forget the way she sobbed as she pressed in against me at that moment.

As I walked back to my car, looking down at my shirt, now stained with tears and mascara, I thought about why I was initially so resistant to following through on what God was prompting me to do. I was struck by the realization that I'm more comfortable asking God to comfort others than I am with having him ask *me* to do it. If I'm being honest, most days I'd rather have God get tear stains and mascara on *his* shirt. I was stung by the conviction that asking God to comfort others was simply a convenient way to avoid getting involved myself.

Strangely Bright

Not long after that car accident, I read a verse from the book of Ecclesiastes that captured my attention: "I observed all the oppression that takes place under the sun. I saw the tears of the oppressed, with no one to comfort them."[1] After reading that, I wondered if perhaps no one was available to offer comfort because everyone was praying for God to do it.

That day in the car, I was torn between an easy Jesus and the real Jesus. The easy Jesus hears our prayers for grieving families and lets us go about our business. But the real Jesus messes with our hearts by asking us to act on the compassion we feel welling up inside us. It's not that feeling pity and praying for someone in need is necessarily wrong. It just isn't complete.

True compassion goes so much further than pity. It layers *action* onto our feelings. Anyone can feel pity, but only the grittiest followers will act on it. The tough decision to live with compassion means choosing to cross the line between feeling sorry for someone and actually doing something about the need.

The Bible presents active compassion as our way of joining God in the restorative work he's already up to in the world. Biblical compassion is a gritty, get-your-hands-dirty, put-your-money-where-your-mouth-is response to real human need. It is fierce and demanding. It strays out of the realm of passive feelings into full-on engagement with other people. Compassion requires reaction.

That's what the world needs—our presence as well as our prayers. People who are struggling and in need aren't looking for pity. They're looking for care and concern that act on their behalf—for people who will not only pray from a distance, but who will also be willing to draw so close to them that our shirts might get stained.

Unfortunately, people don't always get this from the church. Although a lot of Christians are sorry when things don't turn out the way they're supposed to, too few of us are willing to get our hands dirty actually doing something about it.

I think this is partly why Jesus instructs his followers to pray this way:

> May your Kingdom come soon.
> May your will be done on earth,
> as it is in heaven.[2]

In other words, our desire should be that the way things will be done *one day in heaven* will start *right now on earth*.

And if we're courageous enough to join Jesus in praying that prayer, shouldn't we be courageous enough to *work* for it as well? I think so.

When I was growing up, we sang a song that went like this: "Turn your eyes upon Jesus, look full in his wonderful face, and the things of earth will grow strangely dim, in the light of his glory and grace."[3] That sounded good to me. But as I got older, I began to question the idea that our ultimate hope was to detach ourselves from this world, hoping it would grow "strangely dim" in the process. Jesus seems to be more focused on engaging this world, bringing the reality of heaven to earth, redeeming and restoring his creation.

Far from causing the things of earth to grow dim, the light of God's glory and grace illuminates and sharpens our vision of the world. The more we turn our eyes upon Jesus, reflecting on the way he intends for things to be, the clearer our view of the world will become. Our eyes are opened to the sacred potential bursting all around us to experience a small glimpse of heaven right here and right now.

God longs to pour out compassion on the world. And the way he'll accomplish this is through a group of people who are committed to the cause and who aren't satisfied to simply reflect on heavenly ideas, but rather seek to live at the intersection of people's needs and our God-given ability to meet those needs. That's why followers of Jesus should be the most passionately engaged people on the face of the earth. Tapping into God's purpose and plan for the world compels us to stop trying to escape the world—hoping it becomes strangely dim in the rearview mirror as we're zapped out of here—but rather to engage our world, looking for any and every opportunity to react with compassion.

Like all the other tough choices that confront anyone who wants to follow the real Jesus, choosing to act on our compassion shapes us more into the image of Christ. A life of compassion isn't easy, but it's an infinitely better way because there's nothing quite like the experience of tasting heaven here on earth.

Pop Quiz

I hate pop quizzes—well, *all* quizzes—but I'm about to give you one anyway. See if you can pick out the common theme in the three Gospel snippets below. (Don't worry, I'll make it really easy by throwing in some italics.)

Two blind men were sitting by the roadside. . . . Jesus stopped and called them. "What do you want me to do for you?" he asked. "Lord," they answered, "we want our sight." Jesus *had compassion on them* and touched their eyes. Immediately they received their sight and followed him.[4]

A man with leprosy came and knelt in front of Jesus, begging to be healed. "If you are willing, you can heal me and make me clean," he said. *Moved with compassion*, Jesus reached out and touched him. "I am willing," he said. "Be healed!"[5]

A funeral procession was coming out as [Jesus] approached the village gate. The young man who had died was a widow's only son, and a large crowd from the village was with her. When the Lord saw her, his heart *overflowed with compassion*. "Don't cry!" he said. Then he walked over to the coffin and touched it, and the bearers stopped. "Young man," he said, "I tell you, get up."[6]

In each of these situations, Jesus was confronted with a different need. The first two men were blind, which made it hard for them to provide for themselves and probably led to others avoiding them. The man with leprosy was ostracized from society and had likely gone years without being touched by another human. (Just think how isolating that must have felt.) The widow had lost her only son, which meant she now had no male relative to provide for her.

Despite the diversity of these situations, Jesus responded in the same way each time: with compassion. We might say that his heart went out to them, but in the first-century world they had another, even more colorful, way of saying it.

The word translated *compassion* is one of my favorite words from the original Greek of the New Testament. It's the word *splagchnizomai*. (Go ahead and try saying it: splagchnizomai. It rolls off the tongue, doesn't it?)

The word is tied to the idea of one's bowels being moved. Gross, I know. But the connection is actually quite meaningful. In those days, people saw the bowels as the center of one's emotions. So, in the same way that we would say, "My heart's just not in it" or "I got my heart broken," people in the first century would talk about being moved with compassion in their guts.

The point is that Jesus had a visceral reaction when he saw people's needs. It was as if he had been punched in the gut. My guess is that you've had a similar response at some point.

Have you ever come across a person whose situation made you sick to see it?

Have you ever witnessed an argument that took the wind out of you?

Have you ever seen people in pain and something inside you actually hurt *with* them?

There are moments when our gut-level response to something is overwhelming and we can't explain what's driving it. We just know that what we're seeing isn't right. Something inside us is moved. That's splagchnizomai. It's the kind of compassion that wells up inside us and needs a release.

When my daughter was just under two years old, she was flipping through a magazine and something caught her eye. Her gaze was fixed on a picture of a child who had a cleft lip. It was an ad for a humanitarian organization that helps kids who are suffering in this way. An expression of concern washed over Sienna's face. Then she said, "Oh no, boo-boo" and brought the magazine up to her lips to kiss the picture of the child. Even as a toddler, she had an intuitive sense that this wasn't the way it was supposed to be. That sense moved her to want to do something about it. My daughter didn't know it at the time, but what she felt welling up inside her as she saw that picture in the magazine was splagchnizomai.

It's the same punched-in-the-gut reaction Jesus felt when he encountered people's suffering. But *just feeling* compassionate doesn't require any grit. Making the tough choice to convert our compassion into action? That's a different story.

Touched

You may have missed it earlier when you read the three stories from the Gospels, but there was actually a second theme running through those verses. Notice what Jesus did each time he was moved with compassion:

1. Jesus had compassion on them and *touched* their eyes.
2. Moved with compassion, Jesus reached out and *touched* him.
3. When the Lord saw her, his heart overflowed with compassion. He walked over to the coffin and *touched* it.

In each situation, the compassion that Jesus felt stirring him was the catalyst for action. He went to people and did something to help them with their problems. He reached out and made contact. He touched.

Throughout his ministry, Jesus converted emotion into action. He channeled his compassion into specific and deliberate moves to engage the people whose plight had moved him. Compassion drove him to break societal and religious norms in order to engage the people who were in need.

Doesn't our hope rest on this truth? Where would you and I be without a God who was committed to converting compassion into action?

We all were born bogged down by the realities of brokenness and sin. We all were easy prey for temptation, and we've all suffered the effects of wrongdoing—both our own and that of others. We all were cut off from embracing the fullness of God's love.

But God didn't settle for just pitying us in our need. Instead, he acted on our behalf. Our hope is not in a God who simply *feels* compassion. Our hope is in a God who is *moved* by his compassion; a God who *came near* to us and *touched* us in our time of greatest need.

In the words of Eugene Peterson, Jesus "became flesh and blood, and moved into the neighborhood."[7] Theologians call this the Incarnation.

Jesus didn't step into this world only to feel for us, or think for us, or be a model for us. That can all be done from a distance. He came to *touch* the world as well. To get skin to skin with the creation he loves. He came to be with us in our need.

To follow the real Jesus means to become like him in this way, to put skin on our compassion for others by getting involved in their lives, by attacking in tangible ways the things that are wrong in the world, and by working with God to set things right.

God Hates This

The greatest force that keeps us from acting with compassion isn't apathy—it's *religion*. Religion compartmentalizes our faith into safe little expressions of daily or weekly activity. We give our time to a church, read the Bible in the morning, and maybe even tithe—fulfilling our religious obligations in order to distract ourselves from having to consider how we might live out Jesus' incarnated compassion in a needy world. Religion doesn't require us to get our hands dirty. It certainly doesn't call for any grit. It asks us only to pay our dues and check off our boxes, and then it leaves us free to get on with our real lives.

This has been going on in the faith community for centuries—and God hates it.

God hates it so much that he spoke to the nation of Israel through the prophet Amos, warning them against playing the religious game while ignoring the needs of people right in front of them who were hurting:

> I hate all your show and pretense—
>> the hypocrisy of your religious festivals and solemn
>> assemblies.
> I will not accept your burnt offerings and grain
>> offerings.
> I won't even notice all your choice peace offerings.
> Away with your noisy hymns of praise!
> I will not listen to the music of your harps.
> Instead, I want to see a mighty flood of justice,
>> an endless river of righteous living.[8]

Somewhere along the line, the Israelites gave more attention to praying for those in need than to being present with them. They grew content with reaching out to God through their songs and offerings while refusing to reach out to their neighbors.

The Israelites' error is the same one we so often make—channeling all of our energy into religious observance without working to bring about a more just, safe, and healthy life for people in need. We feel pity, as I assume the Israelites did, but simply feeling pity is precisely what enables us to keep singing our songs to God while never doing anything about the needs that are all around us.

Living with compassion is a different story. It requires action. It compels us to get up close and personal with people. We can't practice *presence* from a distance. And we can't outsource presence to God—because he has already *assigned* it to us.

Taking the Gloves Off

Years ago, my friend Rick worked on a floor in a hospital where several patients were dying of AIDS. Part of his job was to attend to these patients by changing out their linens and giving them baths.

He told me one time that he had noticed how, when a patient was nearing death, many on the hospital staff provided *less* care than they had when the patient was in better health. Apparently, it made sense to them to move on to other patients, knowing that the terminal patient would soon pass away regardless.

In particular, Rick described one patient who was in her final days. Everyone knew it, and as usual, the staff became less attentive to her. Near the end, this woman spent large blocks of time alone with her suffering and fear.

One day, Rick walked into her room and went about his job as he did every day. He changed out her linens. He made sure she had what she needed. And then he started to make his way out of the room to move on to the next patient.

But as he reached the door, he looked down at the latex gloves he was wearing and realized that he had never had any interaction with the woman in that room without gloves on.

As he paused in the doorway, he began to reflect on the realities of heaven and how God would want things to be. A question pressed in on him: *Should I reach out to this woman who is dying of AIDS and touch her skin-to-skin?*

Would he act on the compassion he felt welling up inside him, or would he numb it by going about his business? Would he rip compassion out of the realm of good intentions and put flesh on it?

Rick summoned up his grit and walked over to the dying woman's bedside. Removing his gloves, he reached out and took hold of her hand with his.

She looked up at him, squeezed his hand, and said, "That's the first time anyone has touched me without gloves on in over two years."

On earth as it is in heaven.

Three Attitudes of Compassion

Becoming people who act on their compassion requires a change in our thinking. It doesn't come naturally. And it certainly isn't easy. (If it were, everyone would do it.) We must make some conscious and deliberate changes to the way we think about the challenges that other people's needs present to us.

Let me suggest three shifts in perspective that may be

necessary in order for us to move past pity and become people of compassionate reaction when we see a need.

Slow down

Hurrying is the enemy of compassion. It renders us unable to *notice*. We've all hidden behind that smoke screen of hurry, convincing ourselves that if we don't notice, we aren't responsible to act. We've timed things just right on the exit ramp so that the homeless person on the side of the road was only a blur. We've picked up the pace on the sidewalk in order to avoid eye contact. We've quickly changed the subject with people who were sharing about a need or a struggle—or worse, we have cut the conversation short with a token "I'll be praying for you," which, as we all know, is Christianese for "Can we please move on?"

The kind of patience that compassion requires doesn't mean passively waiting around. Rather, it means slowing down enough to notice. It means having the discipline to lay off the accelerator so that you can observe the world around you.

Jesus slowed down enough to notice, but he certainly didn't sit around. He was out walking. He was moving in the towns and in the countryside. And in the middle of his activity, he noticed people.

There is a difference between being busy and being hurried. Busyness has to do with scheduling, appointments, and the clock. Hurry is a mind-set. We can be busy and still take time to notice what's happening around us. On the other hand, we can have an open schedule and be hurried, always looking ahead to what's next, never being in the moment, and conveniently bypassing needs that may present themselves.

Stay busy if you want to, but live unhurriedly.

Expect a mess

I recently watched a documentary called *God Grew Tired of Us*, which is about the Lost Boys of Sudan. In the film, one boy talks about walking down a street, seeing a woman crying on the side of the road, and noticing that nobody stopped to comfort her. So *he* did. He went up to her and in broken English asked her what the trouble was. "When somebody is in pain," he says, "the best way is to go and involve in his problem."[9]

Involve in his problem. That's active compassion.

But let's be honest: Getting involved means we become exposed to the messiness of other people's lives. Addictions are messy. Divorces are messy. Trauma is messy. Depression is messy.

If we are courageous enough to involve ourselves in people's needs, we had better expect a mess. Simple, clichéd answers won't work. Conversations won't be tied up with neat little bows. The needs of others don't take a vacation when we do.

But it's in the midst of the mess that change happens and needs are met. Even our willingness to enter into somebody else's mess is a way of taking off the gloves to get skin-to-skin.

When the boy in the documentary went up to the crying woman and asked what her problem was, he was afraid she wouldn't respond. "I thought she would not accept what I say. But she look at me, and she feel a little bit at home."[10]

If we're prepared to get a little messy by acting on our compassion, the space we create for people will lead to their feeling "a little bit at home."

Make space for interruption

A few years ago, Meghan, one of the students in our church, was preparing for her next steps after high school. She had worked hard to put herself in a position to have options after graduation. She had the grades, the experiences, and the personality that made her an instant *yes* for just about any college admissions team. She ended up having her choice of a couple of colleges she liked.

So there she was in August, packing up some of her belongings, loading up her car, and saying good-bye to her parents. But Meghan wasn't driving to a tree-lined campus in one of America's quaint college towns. She was heading to the airport, on her way to the trash-filled streets of India to work in an orphanage.

Why?

Our church had been mobilizing our community to help the Dalit people, the lowest caste in India, who aren't even considered human by many others in their country. Meghan felt punched in the gut by what she was learning. She couldn't ignore the compassion stirring in her as she heard their stories. She felt compelled by Jesus to go and serve these people. It interrupted her plans, but she was willing to leave behind the normal course of her life to follow Jesus into something unknown.

People's needs are inconvenient—to them and often to us. Each day, we may be given small opportunities to put compassion into action. But it might interrupt our lunch plans or our meeting agenda or the plans we had to clean our home. Sometimes, as they did for Meghan, those interruptions happen on a larger scale. Acting on our compassion may compel us toward a new career path. It may redirect how we thought we'd spend our retirement years.

Pitying someone is so much easier than acting with compassion. But feeling pity for others is not the way of Jesus. It's why compassionate action requires grit. Are you willing to slow down long enough to see the need? Are you okay with stepping into the mess of other people's lives? Will you hold your plans loosely, allowing space for God to interrupt you with his plans to meet the needs of others?

A Little Heaven on Earth

The people around us aren't looking for Christians to *feel* compassionate. But what will grab their attention is a group of people who are committed to *reacting* with compassion, even in the smallest ways.

I realize there is a huge risk in writing about compassion and need. People who work in social service organizations sometimes talk about "compassion fatigue." It's the reaction people have when they say, "I hear what you're saying about how these people need help. But so many people have needs. I've given money, and I've helped people. Right now, I'm just overwhelmed and worn out, almost numb. Check back with me later."

If you've been feeling some compassion fatigue as you've read this chapter, I understand. Between the evening news, the barrage of causes that come through our social media feeds, and the needs of our own families and friends, we often feel tapped out. I get that. And I've been there myself.

I need to tell you that acting with compassion doesn't mean trying to meet every need that comes our way. We're not expected to. It wouldn't be healthy or productive for us to try.

You and I simply do not have the resources or ability to meet every need we see. So, how are we to decide whether a particular need is one we should respond to?

Here's a rule of thumb: When someone's need and your capacity to meet that need intersect, that is the moment for reaction. Sometimes this is in big ways, but most of the time it's in small, seemingly insignificant ways throughout the day. When you feel punched in the gut by someone's pain or circumstances and you have the capacity to do something about it, there's only one thing left to do: react.

So, don't waste time worrying about all the people you can't help. Whom *can* you help?

At some point in your journey, there will be someone by the side of the road for you. It may not be a mother who's lost a child, or a refugee, or somebody who's dying of AIDS;

but there will be a need that stirs up compassion in your gut. And when you find yourself wanting to pray that God will meet the need that you know you have the capacity to meet, make the tough choice instead to convert your compassion into action.

I'm not sure there is anything more rewarding than bringing a little heaven here on earth.

CHAPTER 5

WE ALL BLEED

SEVERAL YEARS AGO, I was taking a flight to California with my family. My two-year-old son, Silas, and I were settling into our seats when I looked over at the man who was seated by the window next to us. He was frail, with sunken eyes and beads of sweat forming on his forehead. He was obviously sick.

As the flight crew prepared for takeoff, the man turned his head, looked across Silas at me, and started a conversation. He spoke slowly, deliberately, as if each word represented a monumental effort of willpower. At times, it was difficult for me to decipher what he was saying, and then he would resort to scribbling words on a pad of paper to help me understand what he was trying to communicate.

He told me his name was Jim, and he asked about my

son and me. He also shared about his own life. He had been a doctor and had worked at UC Davis for years, but now he was a patient, suffering from the debilitating effects of ALS, a progressive and fatal illness commonly known as Lou Gehrig's disease.

Jim was flying home after visiting his brother in Nashville. Jim and his wife (who was sitting in a different row) had made this trip so that he would have an opportunity to say good-bye to his brother in person while he still had some semblance of a voice.

Our conversation broke off after a while, and Jim reached into a bag and pulled out a medical journal to read. As he dragged his red pen underneath each sentence, I could see just how slowly he was able to process what he was reading. I watched this former doctor read and then reread a single sentence four times, and every minute or so, he used his sleeve to wipe his own drool off the page he was reading.

During the last hour of the flight, Jim fell asleep, and my son fell asleep in the seat next to him. As I looked at the two of them, I was struck by the contrast between them. A healthy, thriving young boy, with his whole life in front of him, and the dying man on his way home from saying his final good-byes.

We can't navigate our way through life without confronting the contrasts and contradictions it presents. Wonder, love, and grace surround us. But sitting in the next seat over, only inches away, are suffering, tears, and loss.

We all come from different backgrounds, different economic and social strata, different industries, and different parts of the world; but one thing we all have in common is the experience of pain and adversity. Our pain may be physical, mental, emotional, or spiritual; but no matter the source, the inescapable reality is that we all bleed.

We weren't designed for any of these experiences:

- abandonment
- betrayal
- sickness
- loneliness
- abuse
- neglect
- failure
- loss
- rejection

That's why adversity always takes its toll. For now, you and I live in a world where we are forced to confront the reality of painful circumstances.

Is it possible to experience fullness of life even when the life is being kicked out of us?

Can we remain faithful even when we've suffered betrayal?

Can we find hope even when we've been thrown into the depths of despair?

The improbable answer to all of these questions is yes.

However, fullness of life won't come about by way of an easy Jesus. An easy Jesus will always disappoint us when it comes to facing the deepest pains of life because an easy Jesus is supposed to keep us safe from experiencing wounds or, at the very least, to quickly alleviate any pain.

But the real Jesus never promises to prevent or cure our suffering. Instead, he offers to heal us. That is, although he doesn't always *relieve* our pain, he does *redeem* it. He can make something good out of the most difficult situations, bringing himself glory and bringing us a richness of life in the process.

So the tough choice we face—which will tap into our reserves of grit—is to *own* our pain and then *offer* it to God for redemption. But we will make that choice only *after* we have decided that—despite whatever pain we may have been handed in life—God can still be trusted.

For You

Just hours before he went to the cross, Jesus shared a final Passover meal with his closest followers. Like Jim on the airplane, Jesus knew that his time was nearly up. So after giving his disciples some parting words, he redirected the symbols of bread and wine used for Passover to represent the sacrifice he was about to make—his body broken and his blood poured out for us. Then, when the dinner was over, "they sang a hymn and went out to the Mount of Olives."[1]

I don't know whether you grew up singing hymns or not, but if you did, you might be imagining Jesus and the disciples rolling out of that upper room singing "How Great Thou Art" or "Amazing Grace." But the hymn they sang that night was actually called the "Hallel" (which means *praise*), drawn from Psalms 113–118. Read those psalms, and you'll realize how appropriate the name is.

Jesus had undoubtedly sung the Hallel countless times before. But I can't fathom the newfound significance it must have had for him as he sang these words just hours before his death:

> In my distress I prayed to the LORD,
>   and the LORD answered me and set me free.
> *The LORD is for me*, so I will have no fear.
>   What can mere people do to me?
> *Yes, the LORD is for me*; he will help me.
>   I will look in triumph at those who hate me.[2]

I love those words: "The Lord is for me." That's powerful.

Think about this for a moment: Jesus was about to be betrayed. He was about to be arrested and tried. He was about to be beaten, mocked, and spit upon. He was about to be nailed to a cross and die. He was about to do something that everything in him was screaming for him not to do. And the lyrics that played in his head were, "The Lord is for me."

It was the rock-solid conviction that God ultimately had good in store for him that enabled Jesus to put one foot in front of the other and keep moving through the suffering from Gethsemane to Golgotha. While all evidence around him suggested otherwise, Jesus acted in response to the fundamental reality that God is *with* us, God is *for* us, and God can be *trusted*. Even in the pain.

His courageous decision to trust God didn't deliver Jesus from the cross.

It delivered him *to* the cross.

His pain wasn't relieved, but it *was* redeemed. It led to his resurrection and our salvation.

Let's be clear about what all this means for us.

The easy Jesus, we think, is supposed to deliver us from our pain—relieving it.

But the real Jesus leads us *through* the pain—redeeming it. He causes good to appear where once there was only despair.

But here's what it also means: We will never experience the redemption of our pain unless we are first willing to follow Jesus through it.

Escape Artists

We are by nature pain-averse because pain is . . . well, painful.

Because pain hurts, we will always recoil from it. We will try to avoid it or escape from it in any way we can. Usually, that means either running from it or numbing it. Unfortunately, neither strategy works well over the long term.

When pain comes, our fight-or-flight response kicks in, and flight almost always wins. We run from pain in different ways. We might simply ignore the reality of our pain, denying that it exists or at least refusing to acknowledge the deep effect it has on us. We might try not to think about it, shutting others down when they start to talk about it. We might try to distract ourselves by staying busier than ever, doing anything that will keep our minds occupied and focused somewhere other than on what hurts.

But running isn't the only way we work to avoid dealing with pain. We also escape by numbing. There are entire industries built on offering us the best painkillers money can buy. We are willing to pay top dollar to numb ourselves. But there are cheaper ways to numb our pain as well—more work, more eating, more media. We conveniently distract ourselves in order to avoid dealing with our pain. When it comes to numbing ourselves, we all have our drug of choice.

The problem with running and numbing is that they only work to a limited degree and for a limited time. Because the pain is inside us, it goes with us wherever we go. And all the "painkillers" we resort to eventually wear off, given enough time.

We can choose to run or numb, but our pain will always catch up with us in the end. Like a beach ball forced underwater, it's only a matter of time before it rockets back to the surface.

A Vow That Backfired

A few years ago, a middle-aged woman named Crystal staggered into my office. Within seconds, she collapsed into deep sobbing. I offered her the box of tissues on my desk and waited patiently for her to collect herself.

Eventually, Crystal told me that her life had gone completely off the rails in the past three months. She hadn't paid any of her family's bills during that time—no mortgage, no utilities, no car payment, no credit cards, nothing. However, during this same three-month stretch, she had been spending recklessly, racking up more and more debt. To top it all off, she had hidden everything from her husband. But now he had found out everything, and she was trapped under the weight of her decisions and was on the verge of losing everything.

I asked her how she had gotten to this point in her life.

She explained that, a year earlier, she had been laid off from her job of many years. This had caused her to lose her sense of purpose and identity. She and her husband decided to move to an area of the state where she didn't know anybody, and in the middle of all of these changes, her only child got married and moved away as well. These three life-changing transitions hit her all at the same time, and her response was to act out by impulsively spending their money.

Even though I hadn't met Crystal before that day, I knew there was something deeper that she wasn't telling me. I looked into her red, puffy eyes and said, "Crystal, I hear you. You've undergone a ton of transition in the last year or so. But to be honest, I know a lot of people who have gone through similar transitions and haven't made some of the choices that you've made. It sounds as if these transitions were a trigger for something deeper going on in your life."

She nodded, took a breath, and said, "When I was

growing up, my mother didn't let us have anything extra. She pinched every penny we had, and things were always rigid and tense in our home. But the thing is, we had enough money to afford some of the things we were deprived of. My mother just wouldn't spend it. I feel like she robbed us of joy because she was so tight with the purse strings."

When Crystal was seventeen, her mother died, and that's when she made her life-altering vow. She said to me, "I remember telling myself at my mother's funeral, *I will never live like my mother lived. If I want something, I'm going to get it.* And ever since then, that's what I've done."

So here she was, thirty years later, sobbing in my office because her pain had finally caught up with her. The pain from her childhood had snowballed with the pain of her present circumstances, and she had tried to numb it with "retail therapy." But spending without an income and living for the moment couldn't go on forever.

Running from our pain or trying to numb it will always fail us. But there is another way forward—choosing to *own* the pain rather than trying to escape it. Until we own the pain we've been handed, we can't fully experience the redemption that God wants to send our way.

It Happened and It Hurt

Owning our pain means that we stare down the wounds we've been handed—no matter how big or small the wound may be—and acknowledge that it happened and that it hurt.

My friend Jaime recently spent a weekend with his father because he wanted answers to questions he had been carrying around for years. Most pressing was why his father and mother had divorced when Jaime was eight years old. The first night he was together with his dad, he came right out and asked him: "Why did you divorce Mom?"

At first, his dad was taken aback by the directness of the question. But then he explained how he and Jaime's mother had become increasingly distant as the years went on. They had neglected or refused to talk about the issues that were boiling under the surface, and eventually they became so hardened toward each other that their differences seemed insurmountable. So they decided a divorce was the best way forward.

After explaining all of this to Jaime, his father said, "Honestly, that day your mom drove away for the last time was the best day of my life."

Then my friend leaned in close to his father and said quietly, "You do realize I was in the car with her, don't you?"

When Jaime told me about this exchange, he said, "My dad shouldn't have done what he did. He should have chased after us—after me. But he didn't. And I've been deeply sad about it ever since."

Jaime told me how he was beginning to understand that the rejection he experienced as a child had sent ripples throughout his life that he was still dealing with three decades later. He had become a master at carefully navigating relationships, never allowing people close enough that they could hurt him. As a result, his wife felt detached and distant from him, and his friends wondered why he was always so quick to ask about their lives but never willing to share about his own.

Now, however, he was beginning to come to terms with the reality of what had happened to him. By acknowledging that those wounds ran deep and that he was deeply sad about it, he had taken the first step toward owning his pain. This also became the beginning of healing—for him personally and for those who had been affected by his reactions over the years. For the first time in a long time, he and his wife are now talking openly about how Jaime's sadness has contributed to underlying issues in their marriage. Jaime's wife now understands what drives some of his behaviors, and she is able to respond with more grace and empathy.

There are many reasons why we resist acknowledging our pain. We don't want to admit that something could have that kind of power over us. We've been taught from an early age that part of what it means to be strong is to live above the pain, to be bulletproof, to not let anything get us down.

But glossing over our pain as if it never happened or didn't hurt will never lead us to the fullness of life that Jesus describes. In fact, it can stunt our emotional and spiritual growth. As Frederick Buechner says in his book *Secrets in the Dark*, "If you manage to put behind you the painful things that happen to you as if they never really happened or didn't really matter all that much when they did, then the deepest and most human things you have in you to become are not apt to happen either."[3]

Pain and suffering are as much a reality of life as joy and laughter. We can't experience the wonder of life without also experiencing the wounds. Fullness of life is found in living with both realities side by side. Dismissing our pain or glossing over it robs life of its texture and color. We can't fully embrace the sunniest days without having lived through the stormiest ones. And we can't stand in awe at the true beauty of nature without acknowledging its untamed wildness.

So let's just be honest by saying, "It happened and it hurt," whatever *it* might be. No more numbing. No more running. No more attempts to escape from the pain.

By owning our pain, we take the first big step toward having it redeemed. And once we've stopped running from and numbing our pain, we can begin to offer our stories to others for their healing.

Let Your Wounds Show

Do you remember what Jesus did when he first got back together with his disciples after his resurrection? He showed them his wounds.

It was afternoon on the very first Easter. The disciples were gathered behind locked doors, understandably confused and a bit frightened by the news that Jesus' tomb had been found empty. "Suddenly, Jesus was standing there among them! 'Peace be with you,' he said. As he spoke, *he showed them the wounds in his hands and his side.* They were filled with joy when they saw the Lord!"[4]

One of the disciples, Thomas, happened to be missing from the group on that occasion. As soon as they could, the others told him that they had seen Jesus risen from the dead. But Thomas was skeptical about this. (Come on, don't pretend you wouldn't have been!) So he said, "I won't believe it unless I see the nail wounds in his hands, put my fingers into them, and place my hand into the wound in his side."[5]

Eight days later, Jesus took up the dare. When he appeared again to the disciples, he said to Thomas, "Put your finger here, and look at my hands. Put your hand into the wound in my side. Don't be faithless any longer. Believe!"

"My Lord and my God!" Thomas exclaimed.[6]

What else could he say?

When Jesus showed his wounds, he erased all doubt about who he was.

When Jesus showed his wounds, he removed all fear from the hearts of his disciples.

When Jesus showed the nail holes and the gash on his side from the spear, he not only proved that he was alive; he also proved that our wounds can be healed.

So if Jesus was willing to put his wounds on display as irrefutable evidence of his victory over sin and death, why are his followers so reluctant to show our wounds to others? I believe one of the reasons we've lost credibility in the culture today is that too many of us are unwilling to show our wounds. That leaves the people around us feeling one of three things:

1. They can't relate to the church because it is filled with people who have no wounds and therefore is no place for the wounded.
2. They don't trust the church because they know it is filled with people who do have wounds in life but are covering them up and lying about them.
3. They have no need for a church whose God can't heal their wounds.

When we deny, cover up, or dismiss our wounds, we also deny, cover up, and dismiss the story of our healing, and the thunderous power of the resurrection becomes a hushed whisper in our lives.

It won't be our polished and cleaned-up lives that will convince others of the reality of God's power. It will be our willingness to courageously follow in the footsteps of Jesus by allowing others to see our wounds—by allowing the world to see the scars we carry with us that point to the healing work of Christ in our lives.

How can we introduce others to a wounded Savior while refusing to show them our own wounds? How can we point others to a suffering Savior while playing it safe with our own pain? How can we tell people that they are safe to show their scars if we aren't willing to show ours?

We unlock the potential for healing in the lives of all

the wounded people around us when we grit our teeth and make the tough choice to show them the wounds we've been handed. In the process, we all begin to heal. And we become active participants in the life-giving dynamic of God's redemptive plan.

Me Too

Anne Lamott has an interesting take on how we share our wounds with people. She writes:

> It is not helpful to tell each other cute things we saw on bumper stickers. . . . It is condescending, and patronizing. . . . And yet! Two very short sentences do help, have saved me [more] often [than] I can recount:
>
> The most important is "Me too." Yes, joyous and scared, chosen and lonely, healing and cuckoo, all at once. Yep. Me too.[7]

There are so many people around us who are suffering silently. They don't know that there are others who have experienced the same pain in life but who also have encountered the healing work of God. By showing our wounds, we say to them, "Me too. You do not have to suffer silently or alone."

I believe there is someone in your community who is waiting for you to share your story and show your wounds. There is someone whose doorway to healing will be unlocked when he or she hears you say, "Me too."

When we baptize people at our church, we have someone read aloud the personal stories of the men, women, and students we are baptizing. These stories describe fresh encounters with a fiercely loving God. But then interspersed throughout will be descriptions of loss, heartache, addiction, struggles, and pain that have occurred along the way.

One of the things I love to do while these honest and compelling stories are being read is to look out at the sea of faces in the auditorium. I'm always struck by how many heads I see nodding along. It's as if the crowd is collectively saying, "Me too."

Here are just a few snippets from stories read at our most recent baptism:

"Having experienced physical abuse as a child and then psychological abuse as a young adult, I was at a point in my life where I struggled immensely with anxiety and felt so unworthy of anyone's love, especially our heavenly Father's love."

"My marriage ended just short of thirty years. This was not what I had planned. I was emotionally devastated, scared, and lonely."

"I started to experience severe medical issues. During this time, I also lost my stepdad and my grandfather. This was my breaking point. I became depressed and started having suicidal thoughts. I reached out for help but was turned away. I had never felt so lost and confused."

"I have had a couple of relationship failures since my divorce, and feelings of rejection brought me to the lowest point in my life."

Imagine you've been abused, divorced, chronically ill, depressed, suicidal, or lonely. (Maybe you don't have to imagine. Maybe it's true.) Wouldn't hearing that others have experienced similar pain strengthen your trust that God can redeem your pain, too?

It's interesting to watch what happens when we finally get honest about our stories and are brave enough to offer them for the healing of others: We realize that we're not alone. The more we share our stories, the more heads are nodding. And those who hear our stories are reminded that they are not alone either. Even though the specific circumstances may be different, our stories tie us together because we all bleed, we all have times when we suffer, and we all need an occasional injection of hope. Sometimes all a person needs in order to finally start the journey toward healing is to know that someone else has walked the same road.

We are inspired by success stories. We are moved by rags-to-riches tales. We are challenged by stories of courage. But we relate differently to those who offer up their stories of pain and perseverance. It's through those stories that our spirits are awakened to the possibility of hope and healing.

Join the Club

My friends Abi and Sean lost their daughter Joeli before she was born. I can't imagine how tempting it must have been for them to run from and numb their pain. But they didn't.

Then they heard about a small group in our church made up of people who had lost a child. Abi and Sean once told me that being with that group of friends is "like being in a club that you never wanted to be a part of." But now they can't imagine their lives without it.

Abi told me recently that one of the great things the group did for them was to refer to Joeli by name. She said there were times when other people didn't know what to say about Joeli, since she never made it to full term; but hearing their daughter's name from the others in the group affirmed her identity and acknowledged her worth and significance. It confirmed for Abi and Sean that Joeli had lived. Only a group of people who have bled in the same way would know how healing and redemptive that would be.

It was their way of saying, "Me too."

When I asked Abi why being in that group was so comforting, she said, "Just knowing that we were not alone made such a difference. Knowing that although our story was unique, there were others who had experienced similar tragedies."

As they made the tough decision to embrace their pain by acknowledging that it happened and it hurt, something remarkable took place in their small group: They didn't find themselves wallowing in their pain; they found themselves *healing through it*. The more they owned their pain, the less it owned them. And the wound that had resulted from such a terrible loss as the death of a child eventually stopped bleeding and began to scar over. Though the pain will never completely go away and the loss will always be real, it's no longer an open wound that makes it difficult to face each day. As they've offered up their story to others, their pain has been *redeemed*, though not fully relieved.

Along the way, Sean and Abi found that the redemptive power of their pain spread beyond the members of their original group. They began to actively seek out other couples who had experienced similar kinds of pain, and they offered support, understanding, and compassion as they came alongside these couples and simply said, "Me too."

When I was online recently, I stumbled onto Abi and Sean's Facebook page. It's full of dance videos, pranks that their family plays on each other, and pictures of recent family adventures. The joy in that home oozes through the screen. And interspersed throughout the dance videos and family adventures are pictures of Joeli's gravesite.

Love and loss live side by side in this family's home. Wonder fills their lives because they've made the choice to embrace their wounds as well. The redemption of their pain began with a courageous decision to embrace their suffering, open themselves to others, and say, "Me too." And in those words they hear the echo of another voice—the voice of Jesus—calling out to them, saying, "Oh, you've bled? Me too."

CHAPTER 6

GETTING NAKED
ON THAT OLD
BURGUNDY CARPET

I CAN TELL YOU EXACTLY where I was the first time I saw
a naked woman. It was by a creek in North Carolina when
I was ten years old. Some friends and I were exploring a
wooded lot that sat next to a construction site. While looking for rocks to throw into the creek, I stumbled upon a
weatherworn magazine with the most glorious images my
eyes had ever seen.

We stayed at the creek a little longer than usual that day.

When we were finished looking at those pictures, we did
what the person before us (and probably the person before
that) had done: We threw the magazine back on the ground,
discarding it like a used napkin after a meal.

What I didn't know at the time was that even at that early age, I was learning untruths about sexuality—in particular that bodies are commodities, objects to be enjoyed and then discarded. Real women—with real-life stories, created in the image of God—were reduced to images on a page, to be used and then thrown away with the other trash along a creek bed.

I remember feeling a bit torn that day. Although I was captivated by what my eyes had seen, I felt I needed to hide what I had done. Maybe it was because most of the messages I received about sex growing up were all about *don'ts*.

Don't have sex before you're married.

Don't look at porn.

Don't masturbate.

Don't think "dirty thoughts."

Don't cheat on your spouse.

After all, there was always the remote, yet ominous, possibility that Jesus would return while we were in the midst of one of those activities, and then what? Did you really want to be caught red-handed?

The problem with this guilt-driven perspective is that it completely misses the point. God's ideal for us isn't rooted in a series of *don'ts*. But he also doesn't want us to settle for less than his best for us—that is, for the most intimate of human connections, the ability to know, and be known by, another.

When it comes to our sexuality, the tough choice we face isn't abstinence (though that may be part of it). Rather, it is putting aside our *impulses* in pursuit of true intimacy. And the great reward if we will do this is that we will enjoy a

greater connection than we've ever known and that we'll fulfill one of our deepest, most aching human needs.

Not Good

If we want to really understand sex, we have to go back to the
first words of the Bible.

Genesis starts with an ancient Hebrew poem about a God
who creates a world out of nothing. A God who speaks a
word and turns chaos into order.

The drumbeat to this tribal poem is found in a simple
phrase repeated seven times in Genesis 1:

"It was good."

"It was good."

"It was good."

"It was good."

"It was good."

"It was good."

"It was very good."[1]

But just as we start to settle into the groove, the beat gets
thrown off when we stumble across another simple phrase,
this time in Genesis 2: "It is *not* good."

Here we are, not even a couple of pages into the story of
our origins, when God declares that there is something so
unfit for his creation that it can never be described as good.

Is it sin?

Good guess, but nope.

Idolatry?

Wrong again.

Cats?

I wish.

In Genesis 2:18, God says, "It is not good for the man to be alone."

Loneliness. Separation. Isolation. Not good.

Embedded deep in the fabric of our humanity is the need to be known. The need to connect. The need for intimacy.

It isn't that we aren't *whole* people on our own, but God designed a particular kind of strength and vitality that can only be experienced in the context of human connection to another.

This natural drive for connection and intimacy is so powerful that it often compels people to avoid being alone even when it's to their detriment. Think about what some people (and perhaps you yourself) have been willing to put up with in order to feel connected to others.

- Drinking something that they don't even like just to be in someone else's company
- Compromising their values to maintain a friendship
- Letting themselves be pushed around and walked over by someone
- Enabling destructive attitudes and actions simply to avoid conflict

I had a friend once who kept running back to a boyfriend who was an absolute jerk to her. Looking at it rationally, it was impossible for us to understand why she would do this. But as with most people, her desire for connection and intimacy wasn't driven by rational thought. She didn't like the way he treated her any more than we did. But her fear of being alone far outweighed any momentary pain he caused in her life. Though what she was doing seemed reckless to her friends, she wasn't being stupid; she was just being human.

Known

The first time the Bible refers to sex, the King James Version uses strangely veiled language to describe it: "Adam *knew* Eve his wife; and she conceived."[2] I've always found that funny. As a kid, I thought, *So that's all it takes?*

And yet there's something beautiful about the idea of *knowing* another person. Isn't it, after all, what we long for most—not sex, necessarily, but rather to *know* and *be known*. In the Bible, that level of intimacy has many facets, encompassing the physical, emotional, spiritual, and even sexual aspects of our humanity.

What is sex if not an overt attempt to be connected to another person, to know and be known? But before Adam and Eve went down that particular path of knowing each other, there was a context for their relationship that set the stage. "This explains why a man leaves his father and mother and is joined to his wife, and the two are united into one."[3]

The Hebrew word used in Genesis that communicates the idea of "becoming one" is *echad*. It's the same word used in the traditional Jewish prayer known as the Shema to describe the oneness of God.[4] It's not an image of a casual hook-up, a merely physical connection. It pictures a thorough merging of two into one.

A family member of mine used to work at a lumber company in Georgia that took scrap wood, ripped it into small pieces, and compressed the pieces together with glue to make particle board. It was an incredibly intense process of heat and pressure, but when the process was complete, what had been individual fragments of wood were now one solid board.

That's a picture of what it means to be *echad*—one.

To experience oneness in this way is to bring two individuals together, with all the fragments of their lives up to that point, and place them under the pressurizing heat of lifelong commitment to each other, so that they emerge as one in every way. When a wedding ceremony is over, the couple leaves as one new person: The pieces of their individual personalities, experiences, and gifts are still visible but are so inextricably connected to the other person that we can no longer tell where one begins and the other ends.

And look where it leads—to intimacy: "Now the man and his wife were both naked, but they felt no shame."[5]

That's the power of oneness: to be absolutely secure in the other's love and commitment, so certain of it that we can stand naked and unashamed with each other. No hiding. No anxiety.

And this oneness is expressed and experienced relationally, emotionally, spiritually, legally, and yes, sexually. We can't talk about *being one* without talking about sex. The two are intertwined.

Way More Than Physical

Unwavering commitment is the soil in which *echad* was always intended to grow. And it's that commitment that gives us the confidence that we can stand naked before the other person and feel no shame.

Shame is resistant to intimacy because shame always has its roots in fear. And fear leads to hiding, guarding, and protecting ourselves. So to engage in sex with someone to whom we aren't willing to wholeheartedly commit ourselves in every other way goes against the grain of the intimacy we long for.

C. S. Lewis said that having sex outside the commitment of marriage is like trying to get "the pleasures of taste . . . by chewing things and spitting them out again."[6] We may experience the taste, and it tastes great; but we gain nothing from it—nothing nourishing or life-giving—and thus miss the point. Our taste buds are lit up, but our stomachs are still growling.

Sex outside of marriage is almost a blanket assumption today. Yet this behavior tears at the very fabric of human intimacy and trust. Sex is an expression of oneness—of *echad*—so whenever we have sex with someone without the assurance that he or she is committed to us beyond the moment, we inevitably guard and protect ourselves from getting too close. But even this doesn't keep our hearts safe. Once we become involved sexually with another person, when we expose a vital piece of ourselves with no context or commitment, a question will always rattle around in the backs of our minds: *Will this person still be here for me tomorrow?*

Consequently, there is always a lingering doubt. And doubt produces anxiety and self-protection. As a result, the act of sex, which is intended as an expression of intimacy, actually becomes disconnected from intimacy altogether.

That disconnect can follow a couple into marriage as well. Here's how Tim Keller describes the situation:

> If you have sex outside marriage, you will have to steel yourself against sex's power to soften your heart toward another person and make you more trusting. The problem is that, eventually, sex will lose its covenant-making power for you, even if you one day do get married. Ironically, then, sex outside of marriage eventually works backwards, making you *less* able to commit and trust another person.[7]

The God-given expression of *echad* is within the context of marriage, because in marriage there is a covenant promise, a commitment to each other physically, emotionally, spiritually, and legally. Sex is so much more than the mingling of body parts. It unites us at a soul level with the other person.

You don't have to be remotely interested in the Bible to understand this. Poets, writers, filmmakers, and artists have been trying to express this reality for ages. How many stories have been told about jealous partners, heartbroken murderers, or jilted lovers saying, "I thought you said you *loved* me. But then you left me."

There may be no greater sting to the human soul than to have tasted a bit of *echad*, only to have it ripped away. As a pastor, I am so tired of seeing women's hearts torn to pieces because they gave themselves to some guy who ended up hanging them out to dry. It's no wonder that women speak in terms of having their hearts *broken* and feeling as if they've been *torn apart*. Men often experience the same sort of pain when a relationship that got sexual ends for them. They may express it differently—sometimes even with anger or extreme jealousy—but the wounds are similar.

It's miserable trying to "un-one" what has already been made one. It's like trying to break apart particle board cleanly. Sure, it will eventually split, but not without fragments of wood flying all over the place, leaving behind splintered edges sharp enough to cut.

"Her, Too?"

When I was twenty-one, I spent the summer doing a pastoral internship at a church on Virginia's Eastern Shore. I hadn't been there more than two weeks before all hell broke loose.

One morning, Rob, the lead pastor, asked to speak to

me. He told me that he had been counseling a particular woman in the church over the past several months, and because of this, the two had been spending a lot of time together. Recently, the woman's brother-in-law had become suspicious about her relationship with Rob and had decided to play private investigator. Apparently, he had taken some pictures of them together in the parking lot, but Rob just wanted me to know that there was nothing to this man's suspicions and that the photos wouldn't show anything inappropriate.

"Okay, thanks," I said. I walked out of Rob's office and didn't think much more about it.

About an hour later, Rob called me back in and said, "Well, I want you to know that we did kiss. But just once."

"Okay, thanks," I said, but now I was growing confused and uncertain.

Rob said that he was going home for the day but that he would be meeting with the leadership of the church later to make sure they knew what was going on.

About two hours later, I heard someone banging on one of the doors of the church. When I walked down the hall to investigate, I saw Gina, the lead pastor's fifteen-year-old daughter, sobbing and beating on the door. As I got closer, I could hear her saying over and over again, "He slept with her. He slept with her. He slept with her."

I brought Gina into the office and tried to console her, and before long her mother, Laura, arrived as well. Laura seemed rigidly composed as she told me that Rob was at home and was not doing very well. She asked whether I would go over to the house to encourage him and talk with him.

So I walked over to their house, which was on the church property, and reluctantly knocked on the door, wondering what in the world I was going to say to him.

Rob opened the door and motioned me in without saying a word. As he walked back toward the living room, with me following closely behind, he simply said, "I'm sorry."

After we sat down, he told me what had happened, admitting to an affair with the woman, and we talked about where to go from there. In the middle of our conversation, I looked outside and saw Laura and Gina approaching the house. When I had left the two of them at the church, Laura had seemed calm and settled. But now, as I watched her walking toward the house, I could tell that her demeanor had changed. She looked fierce.

When she came into the living room, she looked Rob right in the eye and said, "I'm going to ask you one question, and you better not lie to me, because you know I will find out. Danielle—*her*, too?" I later found out that Danielle had been Laura's best friend in the community they had lived in before moving to Virginia.

Rob put his head down and whispered, "Yeah, her too."

There I was, a twenty-one-year-old aspiring pastor, standing in the middle of a family that was disintegrating. I was watching a couple that had been made one now splintering into pieces, painfully being un-oned.

Going Back to Not Good

In the Gospels, Jesus uses the context of adultery to weigh in on the topic of sex and oneness. And as you might expect, he pushes the conversation much further.

He starts by reminding his listeners of a rule they have known all their lives. "You have heard the commandment that says, 'You must not commit adultery.'"[8]

Of course they knew that. He was repeating one of the Ten Commandments. It was the law.

An easy Jesus would leave it there—don't have sex with anyone who isn't your spouse—but the real Jesus invites us to make a tougher choice, one that goes beyond just keeping our pants on. The real Jesus expands the conversation on sexuality to include how we *think* about others who are created in the image of God.

"You have heard the commandment. . . . But I say, anyone who even looks at a woman with lust has already committed adultery with her in his heart."[9]

When Jesus warns about lust, it has nothing to do with a prudish stance toward human sexuality. Instead, it moves the conversation about human dignity forward in monumental ways: No person created in the image of God—that's everyone—is ever to be seen as an object to be used.

That's why Jesus caps off this sermonette on lust, sex, and oneness with a stark warning: "So if your eye—even your good eye—causes you to lust, gouge it out and throw it away.

It is better for you to lose one part of your body than for your whole body to be thrown into hell."[10]

Now, before you go grab a knife, let me point something out. Jesus isn't instructing us to literally pluck out our eyes. He knows perfectly well that we can lust even without our eyes. But he's using hyperbole to make sure we don't miss or minimize the intensity and seriousness of his words.

When our longing for *echad* becomes warped and distorted, it has a dehumanizing effect on us and on the people who become the objects of our lust. Lust grabs and takes and exploits.

Lust also schemes. That's why we wait to log on to that porn site until everyone else is asleep. It's why we've learned how to scope and scan without turning our head while we walk down the street. It's why we intentionally place ourselves in situations where we know we'll bump into that person—secretly hoping it will lead to something more.

Sexual sins are private sins. That's part of the allure. They're isolated from the rest of life. How many people do you know who view porn in public? How many affairs are out in the open? Sexual sins always lead us back to where we started: separated, alone. The one thing God said was not good.

If we aren't content to live isolated and separated—if we want the rich and satisfying life that Jesus has waiting for us—we will have to fight for connection. We'll have to commit ourselves to real intimacy—seeking to know and be known in all aspects of our being: physical, emotional, spiritual, and relational. We'll have to fight for connection in our marriages and our families. It won't be easy. It will draw on our deepest reserves of grit.

Finally Naked

When Jenny and I were engaged, there were times when it took every ounce of effort we could muster not to short-change intimacy by giving in to our impulses. There were moments when I didn't think we were going to make it to the finish line of our wedding day. But we did. Our wedding night was filled with our first fumbling attempts at sexual intimacy. It was awkward and beautiful at the same time. And even in all our uncertainty, as we stood naked with each other for the first time, we were unafraid. Just hours before that moment, we had vowed before God and our families and friends that we would be committed to each other for as long as God gave us breath. No matter what might have come our way, we belonged to each other. When you have the security of that kind of commitment, fear and anxiety give way to uninhibited freedom.

What I hadn't anticipated was how the sexual brokenness I carried from childhood would affect our capacity to become one. If you've experienced sexual abuse, you know that your ability to link intimacy and sex is severely jeopardized. I had spent so much energy as a kid trying to disconnect those two realities that trying to piece them back together again could happen only on the other side of a painfully honest conversation with my wife, who refused to let me settle for anything less than *echad*.

About two years into our marriage, Jenny and I finally started getting honest with each other about sex. Up to that point, we'd had plenty of it, but we both knew that the sense of *echad* was lacking at times. Typically, sex was on my terms only. If Jenny initiated, I felt out of control, anxious, and pressured. I don't know how else to describe it, but I felt young and vulnerable, as if I were ten again. My response to the anxiety I felt was to deflect intimacy by getting playful, robbing the moment of any real connection and making it purely physical rather than truly intimate. At other times, I simply ignored Jenny's advances, leaving her alone in her thoughts about why I might be rejecting her. I had worked for years to numb the feeling of being out of control when it came to anything sexual, and I had mastered the art of avoidance.

But I was never really honest with Jenny about any of this. In fairness to myself, I'm not sure that I even understood what was going on inside me. My reactions felt primal; they were not something I was consciously choosing. Still, my anxiety was getting in the way of our relationship and was something we needed to resolve.

One particular night, after I had once again anxiously recoiled from Jenny's advances, she'd had enough. She wouldn't let me hide anymore. It was time to talk. Her fierce love for me wouldn't settle for anything less than living as one. Sometimes we have to demand *echad* from the ones we love. So we sat down on that outdated burgundy carpet in our first home, and she waited me out.

I finally told her something I had never told anyone: I was afraid of her. During sex, I often felt like a passive observer, or else I was overly anxious about how things were going. Often, if I felt she was getting in the mood, I would deliberately pull away from her.

I know that guys aren't supposed to say things like this. I know I'm supposed to say that I was ready to go anytime she wanted. I know I'm supposed to say that the only thing I needed in order to be ready for sex with my wife was the opportunity. I know I'm supposed to make subtle jokes and veiled references to how I naturally wanted to have sex more often than my wife did.

But none of that would be true.

And I've discovered over the years that I'm not alone in this. I can't tell you how many men I know who are scared to death of sex. I'm not talking about being afraid of their biological impulses. That part's easy. I'm talking about *echad*—the naked and unashamed kind of sex. It's that fear of vulnerable connection that drives us guys to trivialize sex by referring to it with slang terminology or flippant humor.

Truthfully, there is nothing—seriously, nothing—scarier than truly intimate sex. It's just you and your spouse standing naked before each other, exposed and vulnerable, open to judgment and critique.

This fear of vulnerability elicits two different responses from us that occur at the exact same time. On one hand, we want to run away and hide. But at the same time, we want to run toward the arms of the one we love—to be embraced, held, and reassured that we are loved just the way we are.

Which is exactly what happened that night we sat face to face on that old burgundy carpet. I handed my raw, wounded self to her and asked her to handle it with care. And she did.

That night wasn't the first time we had sex. But it felt like the first night I had ever truly been naked with Jenny. She and I *knew* each other in an entirely new way. It was the kind of knowing that can only be experienced on the other side of the gritty decision to be vulnerable.

Can we just be honest? Looking at porn would be way easier than having the carpet conversations we need to have with our spouses. And having an affair, where we can enjoy the benefits of a passionate relationship without any of the work—yeah, that might seem easier as well. And yet we wouldn't receive what we long for the most, which is connection at those deepest levels. These other situations won't deliver echad.

If you're married, the specific issues that keep you from enjoying the fullness of *echad* in your marriage may be different from mine. But if you and your spouse commit yourselves to whatever vulnerable work it will take to stand naked and unashamed with each other, I promise you it will be worth it. No matter how long you've been married, together you and your spouse can learn how to experience the oneness that your wedding day promised.

If you're not married, you don't have to fall into the trap

of settling for sex in place of a true connection. Yes, sex is one expression of intimacy, but it isn't the pathway toward it. As a beautiful, strong, and sacred being created in the image of God, you have already been given everything you need to follow the real Jesus into a life of true connection with him and with others. Don't settle for less than his best for you.

A Death That Leads to Life

Recently, I met with Steve and Molly, a young couple who were about to get married. As we talked, the topic of sex came up. They told me that for a while they had done what all their friends had assumed they would do. That is, they were living together and regularly having sex. But then they started coming to our church and gradually became more and more compelled by the life that Jesus was calling them into. They didn't jump in all at once, but they committed to at least continuing to dip their toes in the water of following Jesus. As they did, they began to be confronted with areas of their lives that Jesus was calling them to reconsider, including their sexuality.

One Sunday, on the drive home from church, they talked about what it would mean to stop having sex until the day they committed to each other in marriage. They decided that until they were committed to each other in every way through marriage, they would set aside their impulses in order to pursue intimacy. So they came up with a plan and put it into action.

As Molly sat across the table from me, she was honest about how difficult the decision had been. Of course it was. They had already experienced a watered-down version of *echad*. And yet, she said, ever since they had stopped having sex, she had been filled with a deeper desire for God than she had ever experienced before. She talked about how her desire to pray and engage the Bible had grown as she had worked to develop these practices during times when she and Steve might normally have had sex. Both she and Steve talked about how they could look back now and see how they had used sex as a Band-Aid to cover up the real issues they needed to resolve. Now they were forced to engage with each other emotionally and actually *talk*.

We discussed how the New Testament calls a husband to love his wife as Christ loved the church, which includes being willing to die for her.[11] That's crazy when you think about it—a love so deep that you would be willing to die for your spouse. We talked about how Steve's decision to give up sex for a while demonstrated his willingness to set aside his own desires for the sake of their relationship. It was a type of death—of sacrifice—that he was already willingly entering into, and this would serve them well in their marriage.

As Steve and Molly began to press in to their commitment, they found that Jesus provided answers to questions they didn't even know they had. Questions about intimacy and human connection. Questions about the real purpose and design of marriage. Questions that Molly had about her own worthiness and questions that Steve had about what it means to be a husband.

Following Jesus has healed their relationship and made them whole in ways they didn't even know they needed. But it happened only after Jesus disrupted their lives a bit and raised some issues they needed to resolve.

One thing they discovered along the way was that they wouldn't stop having sex by accident. It would take some grit, some determination, some perseverance. But they believed that *echad*—true connection, true intimacy—was a destination worth pursuing.

In the middle of my conversation with them, Steve said something that struck me. He said, "I know what we're doing is right. And I know it's good."

Good is worth fighting for.

And what's not good is worth fighting against.

I wish I could tell you that pursuing *echad* has been easier for me since that conversation on the carpet, but most days I still find myself having to fight, scratch, and claw my way toward it. But I'm as convinced as ever that it's worth the fight. As all good things are.

CHAPTER 7

LOWERING AND LIFTING

ONE NOVEMBER MORNING a couple of years ago, a man walked into a local bank, cashed a check made out to himself, and left with a wad of cash. Only later was it discovered that he had withdrawn more money than he had in his account. I heard about this from the branch manager, Steve, who is a member of our church.

Steve immediately closed the customer's account and started trying to find him. But after leaving several voicemail messages, e-mails, and texts with no response, Steve thought the bank would never see the man again.

Later that week, however, the same customer walked into the bank and tried to withdraw some more money. When he was told that his account had been closed, he became irate and started screaming at the teller.

Steve intervened, pulled this man into his office, and explained the situation to him.

"Because you wrote a fraudulent check, we terminated your account. That's bank policy. It's also bank policy for me to call the police and report this as a criminal offense."

When the man heard this, sorrow washed over his face. It was as if for the first time he really understood what he had done.

At the same moment, Steve's heart opened up to the possibility that God was interrupting his plans with an opportunity to serve this man. So Steve did something that wasn't written anywhere in the bank's policy manual. He said to the man, "Tell me what's going on in your life that has led you to this point."

He found out that, within the past year, the man—whose name was Jon—had lost a leg because of a medical condition. The medical procedures he needed had left him buried in debt. He was alone in life and felt as if he had no chance of ever getting out of the suffocating situation he was in. As a result, he found himself doing things he never thought he would do—such as writing fraudulent checks just to get by.

Steve decided not to call the police about Jon, but he knew he needed some time to consider the best course of action and to figure out what God was stirring up in his heart.

A few days later, which happened to be Thanksgiving, Steve decided to give Jon a call.

"How are you spending the holiday?" he asked.

"I'm not doing anything," Jon replied.

"We've got a lot of extra food here," Steve said, "and if it's okay with you, my wife and I would love to bring you a plate and spend some time with you."

Jon took him up on his offer, so Steve and his wife packed up some food and spent the next few hours at Jon's place, eating together, talking, and getting to know a man whom many people might have written off.

Toward the end of their conversation, Steve asked Jon if he would be interested in going to church with them.

Jon said, "Who's going to let a one-legged bank defrauder into their church?" (Isn't that the greatest question ever?)

Steve responded confidently, "My church will."

The very next Sunday, Steve took Jon to church for the first time. They sat together, encountering a God who loves both the defrauders and the defrauded.

Now think back to the moment when Steve first met Jon at the bank. Steve's position as branch manager gave him all the power and authority in that situation. And the question that began rattling around in his heart was, how would he *use* that power and authority? The most practical and obvious response would have been to follow the letter of the law and call the police. Banks don't like to lose money, and Steve would have scored some points with his employer by enforcing the rules and reclaiming what was lost. It might have even counted in his favor at his next performance review. But Steve chose a different path.

Make no mistake: Steve didn't forfeit his power and authority. He simply chose to use it for something other than his own self-protection or advancement. He decided to leverage his authority for the ultimate good of a "one-legged bank defrauder."

The thing is, if Steve had been riding with an easy Jesus, he might have missed the opportunity altogether. Easy Jesus doesn't distract us from pursuing our own ambitions. He's a nice traveling companion on the road trip of life, but he would never interfere with our dreams, our definition of success, or our goals. He certainly would never question whether what we're pursuing is actually worth it. He's along for the ride, but we always get to drive.

But people like Steve have discovered that a Jesus who just rides shotgun as they pursue their own ambitions really isn't Jesus at all. They're in the process of learning that the tough decision to put God's Kingdom ahead of their own goals and dreams leads to more true fulfillment, paradoxically, than any amount of self-aggrandizement or self-protection ever could. They've come to understand that all the grit and energy they invest in serving others in the name of Jesus redefines their perception of greatness.

What Do You Want to Be When You Grow Up?

When my daughter, Sienna, was about three years old, she asked me a question out of the blue one day: "Daddy, what do you want to be when you grow up?"

"A pastor, I guess."

"You do that now," she said. "What about when you grow up?"

Touché.

What struck me most about our conversation was where Sienna took it next. She went on to tell me about her own desires, articulating in great detail what she wanted to be when she grew up.

Do you remember daydreaming as a kid about what you would do someday? (By the way, I always thought I'd be a pilot.) Have you ever thought about why kids do this? It makes no practical sense. They have no reason to give their future work a single thought. When you're a kid, everything is handed to you—literally on a plate, at times.

And yet that isn't enough. Every child, even at a young age, has strong ideas about what he or she wants, and kids always want to do things their own way.

I can't tell you how many times my kids, when they were toddlers, fought and kicked and screamed and tried to escape from the stroller while we were out somewhere. They mastered the little trick of transforming their bodies into a Jell-O-like substance, enabling them to slide down the front of the stroller until we inevitably ran over them as we would a puddle.

I tried reasoning with them: "You are getting a free ride to your destination. You literally don't have to do anything except enjoy the ride. You will never have it this good in life again. So why in the world are you so intent on getting out and walking?"

My pleas fell on deaf ears. They wanted to go where *they* wanted to go, and they wanted to do it under their own power.

We are helpless to resist the urge to move forward, to grow, to walk on our own, to do things we've never done before or make things that nobody but us could make. It's as if we're hardwired with an urge to do something in this world and to leave our mark. Just sitting in the stroller while someone else pushes us along isn't going to cut it.

The question of what we want to do with our lives has no less significance for us as adults than it did when we were kids. Even if the busyness of life, the setbacks and disappointments we've experienced, and the humdrum of everyday living has muted the urges within us to do things that matter, we are nonetheless driven by a longing for meaning, purpose, and significance.

How could we not be?

We were created for glory.

This Is Heavy

Glorious is an adjective we don't use much anymore. At least not in the circles I run in. When we do use it, it's typically to describe an object or an event—as in "That sunset was glorious" or "That was a glorious sermon you gave today." (No, I've never actually heard that last one, but hey, I can dream, right?) We rarely hear the word *glorious* used to describe another person. When was the last time you described your children as glorious? Or your spouse? Or your boss?

Glorious feels like too lofty a word to describe people. But listen to how Psalm 8 describes what it means to be human: "When I look at the night sky and see the work of your fingers—the moon and the stars you set in place—what are mere mortals that you should think about them, human beings that you should care for them?"[1]

At first, we're tracking with the psalmist because we've all had the same experience of wonderment. We just spend a minute under the expanse of the stars or stand at the edge of an ocean, and we can't help but acknowledge the seeming insignificance of the human race. But then the psalmist continues: "Yet you made them only a little lower than God and crowned them with *glory* and honor."[2]

As small as we may feel, we are *glorious*!

The Hebrew word for glory carries with it the idea of weightiness or heaviness. If we were to walk outside right now and drop a heavy stone onto soft soil, it would have an observable effect on the ground. Likewise, to be crowned with glory is to be filled with the potential to leave a noticeable mark on the soil of our lives.

God has loaded us up with divine desires to make a difference in this world—among our families and friends, in our communities, and in the work we do each day. Our glory is the sacred combination of everything about us that gives us weightiness in the world—our passions, our strengths, our intelligence, our skills and experience, our unique perspective on the world, and our assets and resources. All of it makes up our glory. We were created to do big things.

But don't get me wrong. When I talk about doing big things, I don't mean becoming famous, writing bestsellers, topping the charts, advancing to the top spot at work, or filling up our bank accounts. Certainly, God may allow us to accomplish such things; if so, be assured that they are good. But living big lives isn't about being recognized or how much we accomplish. In fact, we could receive tons of recognition for the things we've done and yet still live small lives of little impact. The question is how we will leverage the unique glory that we've been given.

If you've ever seen kids playing dress-up, you know they aren't big enough to fill out the adult clothes they're wearing. That's what we look like when we try to put on a glory that isn't ours. But God has gifted each one of us individually—calling us into the good works that he has uniquely designed each of us to walk in.[3] All we've been asked to do is to fill out the clothes we've been given.

The question isn't whether we have a unique capacity to make a mark on the world. If we are still living and breathing, that issue has been settled because we've been crowned with glory. It's in us. The question now is simply what kind of world we will build with that glory.

Make Something of It

As we continue to read in Psalm 8, we find that our glory has been given to us for a reason: "You gave them charge of everything you made, putting all things under their authority."[4]

These words are an echo of Genesis 1:26-30, where we're told that God created humanity in his own image.

To be created in the image of God means that we have the unique capacity to rule and reign over the world on God's behalf.[5] That's why God placed the first humans in the Garden of Eden and told them to tend and watch over it.[6] Today, we still have a responsibility to tend the "garden" of this world, creating things of beauty and value.

A garden starts as a patch of dirt. But after we cultivate, plant, and care for the garden, something happens. What was once a patch of dirt is now teeming with life. Gardens don't happen by accident, and neither does the future. We have been crowned with glory, created in God's image, to create the future alongside him.

That's why we feel a sense of fulfillment after we solve a complex problem at work, organize our homes, or type the final word on a manuscript. What comes to life at those times is our innate desire to rule and reign, to create good work, and to bring order to the world in the unique ways that we've been equipped by God. It's the image of God showing through.

In *Christ the Lord: The Road to Cana*, Anne Rice's novelized version of Jesus' early life, someone asks Jesus why he is a carpenter. He responds, "The world's made of wood and stone and iron, and I work in it."[7]

Jesus was engaged in the ordinary work of this world. Likewise, you and I have been created in the image of God and crowned with glory, not so that we can escape the everydayness of our world but so that we can fully engage it. We bring our full selves—our glory—to bear as we work with computers, create spreadsheets, make coffee, help kids with homework, design clothes, lead meetings, pour concrete, or hang drywall. This is where the world is for us: fresh plots of soil that we've been given to make something of.

We can no more shut down our aspirations than we can remove the God-given crown of glory from our heads. But will we channel our glory for our own advancement and advantage, or will we use it to fulfill God's purposes for the world by serving others who also have been created in the image of God?

How we answer that question marks the fundamental difference between humility and pride.

Among You It Will Be Different

There is nothing more dangerous than when pride hijacks our glory and our aspirations become arrogant attempts to build our own world. When our aspirations to live weighty lives dissolve into arrogance and ambition, we forget that it was God who gave us those desires in the first place, and the glorious energy that God gave us to build his Kingdom becomes twisted and warped. This was the underlying issue in one of the more intense recorded conversations between Jesus and his disciples.

Jesus was on his way to Jerusalem and for the first time talked plainly to his disciples about the bloody fate that awaited him there. After Jesus was done describing the horrible scene into which he was willing to walk for the sake of humanity, two of his close followers, James and John, decided it was the perfect time to ask Jesus for a favor. They said, "When you sit on your glorious throne, we want to sit in places of honor next to you, one on your right and the other on your left."[8]

Somewhere along the way, James and John's idea of glory had been distorted by pride. They thought that glory was about being in charge, getting recognized, and having power for power's sake. They wanted people bowing in their presence. They had in their minds the kind of throne that Jesus was marching toward as they traveled to Jerusalem, and they wanted to be enthroned along with him.

But what they hadn't yet come to terms with was that the "throne" Jesus was marching toward wasn't made of gold. It was made of wood. And he would not climb onto this throne; he would be nailed to it.

This was a story about power, honor, and strength, and the two distinct paths one can take toward greatness.

Jesus responded, "You know that the rulers in this world lord it over their people, and officials flaunt their authority over those under them. But among you it will be different."[9]

When we describe people as "throwing their weight around," it's typically not a positive statement. It means they are using their power and their position to get what they want. That's what the "rulers in this world" do—throw their weight, their glory, around.

We all have authority in some realm of life, whether it's with the kids we are raising, in the classes we teach, in the companies where we work, in our neighborhoods, or with our friends. We live in a world where the expectation is that we will use our platform, power, and influence for our own glory.

And that's always the temptation, isn't it?

To lord over people any influence and power we may have.

To throw our weight around to promote our own interests.

To bring ourselves recognition.

To make ourselves look good.

To take our rightful seats on *our* thrones.

It's why Lucifer got the boot from his place in heaven and why Adam was tossed out of the Garden. There's nothing original about it. It's a tale as old as time. And it's why God indicted his people through the prophet Jeremiah: "My people have changed their glory for that which does not profit."[10]

Not long ago, I sat down with a new friend named Josh and asked to hear his story. He started talking about his upbringing.

It seems that Josh's father was incredibly successful in his career. Just about everything he touched turned to gold. As a result, he was given more and more responsibility at work. Josh couldn't pinpoint when it happened because it was such a subtle shift, but somewhere along the line he realized that his dad was away from home more days than he was there.

I asked Josh, "So, how many days out of the year was he away?"

"Well, during my sophomore year in high school," he said, "I saw him a total of three weeks, I think."

My mouth hung open for a second, as I thought I'd misheard him. But I hadn't.

"And the other years of high school weren't that different. He never saw me play football. He never knew my friends or my struggles. I lived my whole life without him noticing."

And then, as if trying to let his father off the hook, he said, "But I get it. He had a lot going on with work, and he was making a lot of things happen there. He was great at what he did."

I'm sure Josh was right—no doubt his dad was great at what he did on the job. But when you stack those accomplishments against the price of not knowing his own son, it's easy to conclude that he had become great at things that did not profit.

When our glory is hijacked by our ambition, what often gets left behind in our pursuit of the next promotion, bonus, or bit of recognition are important relationships with others, such as our families and friends.

When our desire to live weighty lives gives way to greed, the people around us become obstacles or pawns to be used in our pursuit of more.

When we trade our glory for comfort, the willingness we once had to take risks and to be open to the leading of the Holy Spirit is co-opted by complacency, and our capacity for true greatness grows stale with inactivity.

But Jesus said, "Among you it will be different. Whoever wants to be a leader among you must be your servant, and whoever wants to be first among you must be the slave of everyone else."[11] The implication here is that there's a tough decision for us to make.

We can choose to use our power, influence, and authority—all the weight we've been given—to lord ourselves over people. Placing them under our command. Using others to prop up our dreams and advance our glory.

That's easy. In fact, it's expected. But Jesus wants to save us from that path because it won't lead to life in all its fullness. (Just ask my friend Josh.)

Thankfully, there is another way. To everyone who doesn't want to settle for an easy Jesus, the real Jesus says, "Among you it will be different." The gritty choice he asks us to make is to humbly leverage our glory in service to others.

The Way of a Servant

A few years ago, my wife spent an afternoon with a group of women who own a beauty salon in Phnom Penh, Cambodia. These are skilled businesswomen who know how to make money and run an organization with the best of them. Their salon has a great reputation, the seats are almost always filled, and the cash register is constantly ringing.

When you consider how poor their country is, these women could be tempted to accumulate as much money for themselves as they can. They could lord it over others, flaunting their comparative wealth and devoting every possible hour to making more money and expanding their business empire.

But that's not how they roll.

Instead, they use their experience and skills to help girls who have been rescued from the sex trade—some as young as nine or ten years old. They bring these girls in and give them jobs in the salon, teaching them skills they can use to generate income and get out of poverty. They give the girls safety and shelter by using their profits to secure housing for them. They spend time with the girls, shoulder to shoulder, restoring their dignity and their sense of worth.

Yes, they run their salon to generate as much profit as they possibly can. They know that the more profit they make, the better they are at business, and the more excellent they are at their work, the more ways they can serve these girls in need.

I have a friend who has had more sick days in his life than well days. He also happens to be a great musician. So he works as hard as he can to write honest songs about pain and longing and God's redemption in the middle of it all.

Does he want as many people as possible to sing his songs? Yes. Why wouldn't he? Humility doesn't mean he needs to let those desires go. It simply means that he takes those desires and offers them for the good of others.

It's the way of a servant. The way of the Cross. There is always a cross involved in humility, because humility means that we die to our own desires as we seek the good of someone else. That could be as simple as sacrificing an extra hour we have on a Saturday or surrendering our plans for how to spend our money or setting aside the plans we made for retirement.

Every time we choose the path of humility, our pride dies a little more. That's why Jesus finished his conversation with James and John by saying, "Even the Son of Man came not to be served but to serve others and to give his life as a ransom for many."[12]

God is a servant.

Think about how ridiculously scandalous that idea is.

All of God's glory, every ounce of it, is given in humble service to us.

So when we live humbly, lowering ourselves to lift up others, we paint a picture for the world of who God is and what he is like. We believe that God, in Jesus, is putting the world back together again, fixing what is broken, healing what is hurt. And we believe that we can join in this grand plan of God's renewal of the world, starting with our own lives.

When we lower ourselves to lift up others, living humbly as servants, it is our way of saying to the people around us, "There is a God of love who has lowered himself to lift you up. Want me to prove it? Let me serve you."

Tables Waiting to Be Waited On

Take a moment to think about the glory you've been given: your unique passions, strengths, gifts, personality, resources—

all the things that give you weightiness and influence. Write some of those words down in the margin of this book if you need to.

Now think about how you could practically leverage your God-given glory today to lift up someone else.

I hope your mind will be flooded with ideas of ways you can serve others. As you look for opportunities to lower yourself in order to lift up others, my advice to you is simple: *Think small in order to live big.*

The word for "servants" in the New Testament refers to someone who waits on tables. I love that image because it's doable. It's not quitting your job and going into full-time ministry. It's not eradicating poverty in some emerging nation. It's just waiting on tables. Anybody can do that.

There's nothing wrong with doing dramatic works in far-flung places. But you don't have to start there (or even end up there). You can start small. You can start in the place where you are right now. You can start by opening your eyes to the ordinary people, and their ordinary needs, surrounding you today. Your friends, family, neighbors, and coworkers all are "tables to be waited on." What can you do today to lift them up and advance their good?

Building our own little kingdoms will never deliver the contentment and fulfillment we experience when we build God's Kingdom instead. When we build our own kingdoms, we find ourselves living with a sense of entitlement—after all, we earned it, right?—and we constantly compete with anyone who threatens our kingdoms, anxiously looking over our shoulders at whoever might be coming up from behind to surpass us.

But when we lower ourselves to lift up others, the light of joy begins to seep through the cracks in our lives, illuminating the dim corners of our hearts. We taste a bit of glory—the kind of glory that comes from taking our best, most powerful, and most creative parts and offering them up for the good of others—and it tastes *good*.

When it comes to serving, start small. Because if you think too much about serving in big ways, you may miss the tables that are right in front of you, and you may miss the rewards that can come only on the other side of humbly using our glory for the good of others.

Everyone on Equal Ground

A few years ago, our church took a large group of middle school students to serve at a local homeless shelter. The kids cleaned up the cafeteria, served meals, sorted clothes, and helped organize the food closet. Right in the middle of all the activity was Kelly. She was twelve, but she functioned at about a third-grade level because of the effects of a disease that had stunted her physical, emotional, and intellectual development. Kelly had been a part of our church for several years, and everyone knew who she was because she was different. Her speech was slow; she struggled to articulate the ideas that flooded her young mind faster than she could form the words; and when she did speak, spit flew from her mouth.

Kelly was also one of the most loving girls around. Nobody could give a hug quite like Kelly. At our church, she found love and acceptance, and she was able to express her love in return.

That day at the homeless shelter, when I looked over and saw Kelly humbly serving alongside all the others, I caught a glimpse of something beautiful. Next to Kelly was a typical eighth grader—strong, still growing, and full of potential. Next to him was a kid from a wealthy family. And next to that kid was a girl from a poorer family. But there they all were, side by side on their knees, sorting through canned goods together. Everyone was on equal ground as they lowered themselves, kneeling together in humility.

Kelly will never be the smartest, most articulate, or most successful. But in God's Kingdom, those rungs on the ladders don't apply.

And that's what I witnessed that day as I watched Kelly, and those serving next to her, offering all of themselves to advance the good of others: a glimpse of the Kingdom.

They shone. Brilliantly.

Among them, that day, it was different.

And it was glorious.

CHAPTER 8

ENOUGH

ONE DAY, when my daughter was three years old, I walked into her bedroom and noticed that she was intensely counting some items on her bed. As I got closer, it appeared as if a Silly Bandz bomb had exploded across her bedspread. (In case you don't know, Silly Bandz look like colorful rubber bands when stretched out, but they then contract into the shapes of animals, letters, and other kid-pleasing figures.)

There was Sienna, counting all her Silly Bandz as if they were rubbery pieces of gold. I think she had more than fifty when it was all said and done. Then she pulled them on, over her wrist, one at a time, until there were so many that it formed a Silly Bandz sleeve on her short little arm.

When she was finished, she looked at me with the utmost intensity and passion and said, "What I need are more Silly Bandz."

I didn't know quite how to respond.

Before I could whip out a sermon on the evils of greed, it struck me that we all have Silly Bandz that we've convinced ourselves we need more of.

- *What I need are more tools.*
- *What I need is a nicer car.*
- *What I need is a better kitchen.*
- *What I need is an upgraded wardrobe.*
- *What I need is an exotic vacation.*

The first home that Jenny and I bought was a two-bedroom place with maybe a thousand square feet of space. We loved that home. But after we had our first child, we started growing restless. The word *enough* began creeping into more of our conversations, as in "I'm not sure this place is big enough for us anymore. What we need is more space."

Around that same time, I had an overseas trip. On the way home, I was seated next to a young woman from Taiwan. We started talking about our lives and our families, and I pulled out my laptop to show her some pictures of the town where I lived. She had never been to the United States and seemed fascinated by what I showed her. Then a picture of my house popped up on the screen—my two-bedroom, no-front-yard, not-big-enough-for-three house.

She looked at it and then said in broken English, "Whoa! Is yours?"

"Yep. That's my house."

"Wow! Really, really big."

I guess "enough" is relative.

Think back ten years ago to what you had in your life at that time. The car you drove. The vacations you took. The kitchen you had. The house where you lived. It all worked, right? Yet those very same things that satisfied you back then don't quite seem to get the job done now. Fifty Silly Bandz were good enough once upon a time, but now it takes a hundred.

Unless something radical happens in our hearts, enough is never going to be enough for us. Contentment will always recede like the tide in front of us as we pursue more, more, and even more.

What if, instead of being dissatisfied with how much we have, we became dissatisfied with how much we were able to give? What if we organized our lives around generosity rather than consumption?

I know—easy Jesus doesn't intrude on our bank accounts or mess with our assets. He's cool with an occasional contribution to a local charity or church. But beyond that, he isn't all that concerned with how we use the resources we've been given. That's what makes him so easy. The only problem is that I don't find that Jesus when I read the New Testament—as much as I would like to.

If we want to follow in the footsteps of the real Jesus, we'll have to make the tough choice to open our tightly clenched fists and give generously from our resources.

The decision to step through the narrow door of increased giving, even when everything in us tells us to grab more for ourselves, will bring within reach the contentment we desire. The more loosely we hold our possessions, the less they will possess us. The more we give, the more we will find that what we have is truly enough. And the rewards we receive from seeing other people's lives improved will fill our own lives with a richness that can't be contained in a bank account.

Still, the decision to live generously will require massive investments of grit because we'll have to trust God that, if we give today, he will provide for us tomorrow.

Maggots in the Manna

When Moses led the people of Israel across the Red Sea, they found themselves in one of the most barren and hostile places in the world—the Sinai Desert. Where was their water going to come from? Where were they going to get food?

God was about to use these circumstances to teach them a profound lesson about trust and contentment.

One morning, the Hebrews awakened to find a flaky substance all over the ground. They'd never seen it before. As they looked at it with quizzical expressions, some guy in the back yelled out, "Hey, I know what we should do. Let's try eating it!"

Despite having no clue what they were eating, they liked

it. So they asked Moses, "Hey, what is this stuff?" (Hence the word *manna*, which means "what is it?")

Moses replied, "It is the food the LORD has given you to eat. These are the LORD's instructions: Each household should gather *as much as it needs*."[1]

I can't imagine how difficult those last words must have been to take seriously. As much as a household needs? The line between *want* and *need* can be fuzzy, especially when your stomach is growling. And who knew if they'd be hungry again in an hour?

Moses gave the people a starting point and told them to pick up about an *omer* (two quarts) per person:

> The people of Israel did as they were told. Some gathered a lot, some only a little. But when they measured it out, everyone had just enough. Those who gathered a lot had nothing left over, and those who gathered only a little had enough. Each family had just what it needed.[2]

It seems that God wanted his people to learn that he would provide each family just what they needed. And that would be enough. But you know how it is—people inevitably begin to want more than just enough. (A few more Silly Bandz on my wrists would look awesome, right?) So some of the Hebrews gathered more than their families could eat in a single day.

It probably made sense to them to plan ahead and work

harder to prepare for an uncertain future. After all, there was no guarantee that the flaky stuff was going to be there again tomorrow. Why not grab what they could today?

But as they quickly learned, stockpiling manna was a huge mistake. Those who "didn't listen and kept some of it until morning" woke up the next day to find that it "was full of maggots and had a terrible smell."[3]

Isn't that how it goes with our money and possessions? Our purses develop holes, thieves break in and steal, and moths destroy what's left.[4] Inflation and taxation eat away at the value of our savings. Investments go south. The housing market dips, and our mortgages go underwater.

The security provided by material wealth isn't what it's cracked up to be. We know this. Still, we grab as much stuff as we can when we can get it.

Last year, I decided to pay attention to all the Christmas ads that were sent to my house. From October until mid-December, I took every Christmas promotion and advertisement I received and stacked it neatly in the garage. In just under three months, I accumulated an enormous pile of colorful ads, all making their pleas for me to spend money at their stores.

Here were some of the taglines I found on these ads:

"For a limited time . . ."

"One time only . . ."

"Biggest sale ever . . ."

Do you really believe any of those statements? Of course not. We all know that next year's sales will be the new "biggest one ever" and that the "limited time" deal will come back around soon enough—if not at one store, then at another.

Yet these words create a visceral response in us. They play to our embedded fear that if we don't buy it now, we won't have it for tomorrow. Better save some manna for breakfast.

Some people see the world through a lens of scarcity, believing that there is a limited amount of resources and there won't be enough for everyone. So we'd better get ours while we can and then hold on to it for dear life, because we may not have access to it again.

For the Israelites, the consequence of grabbing and hoarding was maggot-filled bread. For us, it goes much further.

Bad Eyes and French Fries

Jesus talked a lot about money. Out of the thirty-eight parables he told, sixteen were about how to handle our money and possessions. In fact, in the Gospels alone, one out of ten verses deals directly with the subject of money. Compared to roughly five hundred verses on prayer in the Bible, and fewer than five hundred verses on faith, there are more than two thousand verses on money and possessions. So it's safe to say that what we do with what we have is kind of a big deal to God.

At one point Jesus said, "Wherever your treasure is, there the desires of your heart will also be."[5] Whenever Jesus refers to our "heart," he's talking about the place where all our attitudes, behaviors, emotions, energy, and affection come from. It's a really simple principle: Our hearts always follow our treasures. If we allocate our treasure to the Kingdom of Me, that's where our hearts will be. If we allocate our treasure to the Kingdom of God, then *that's* where our hearts will be.

Jesus gave an ominous warning about the outcome of putting all our treasure in the Kingdom of Me:

> Your eye is like a lamp that provides light for your body. When your eye is healthy, your whole body is filled with light. But when your eye is unhealthy, your whole body is filled with darkness. And if the light you think you have is actually darkness, how deep that darkness is![6]

In the ancient world, people believed that the eyes were windows to a person's soul, revealing what was happening deep inside. Having "unhealthy eyes" was a metaphor for being corrupted on the inside—the kind of deep-seated corruption that would cause us to grab and hoard. This inner corruption would naturally affect the way we see the world.

I used to live next door to a guy named Tyler, who did detailing work on cars. So when he offered to clean my Jeep, I was thrilled. I paid him to wash the car, make sure its tires looked great, and basically make everything look shiny and new.

Where he really earned his money was on the headlights. Somehow they had developed a hazy film that dampened the beams, though I had never really noticed it.

Tyler started working on the headlights around three o'clock that afternoon. When I looked out my window around four, he was still working on those headlights, scrubbing them with every ounce of effort he could muster.

A few minutes later, he asked if he could take the Jeep to his shop in order to buff out the haze. When he returned, the headlights looked brand-new.

That night, when I went for a drive, I couldn't believe what I saw in front of me when I turned on the headlights. I saw the road, and every little detail jumped out at me in the brighter beams cast by my newly cleaned headlights. I hadn't realized how dim they had become.

Our eyes can go bad without our knowing. When our vision gradually fades over time, we adjust and get used to seeing the world in diminished ways. Likewise, it's possible for our treasures—our money and possessions—to become so much of who we are that we begin to see the world in warped and distorted ways.

Jenny and I spent some time in Asia a few years back. On the first day of our trip, we were in Cambodia and we joined a group of people at an open-air restaurant. Since we weren't quite ready to dive into the local cuisine too quickly, we settled for hamburgers and fries.

As we were wrapping up our meal, four boys came off the street and made a beeline for our table. They wanted to know if we would buy some cheap picture postcards they were selling.

We happened to be dining with a woman who lived in that city, and she warned us not to give the boys any money. More than likely, she said, there was a man somewhere nearby watching to see whether the boys got any money, and he would force them to hand it over to him. Sure enough, we looked across the street and spotted the man who had sent the boys over.

We kept telling them that we were not interested in buying their postcards. But as we were talking, we noticed that the boys were staring at the leftover food on our table.

They were starving.

When Jenny asked them if they'd like the rest of our fries, they nodded enthusiastically. So we loaded them up, and they went on their way.

A few minutes later, as we were getting up from the table, another Westerner walked straight toward us. He got about eight inches from Jenny's face and said in a voice dripping with disgust, "Do you want to know what those little boys did after you decided to give them your fries? They came to my table and asked me for mine!" Then he turned around and walked off.

When your French fries are more important to you than the hungry kids standing in front of you, your eyes have gone bad. You're seeing the world in distorted ways.

My guess is that you'd never think you would choose some cold French fries over a hungry child. And you probably wouldn't. But there are a thousand other signs that our eyes have gone bad when it comes to our money and possessions.

- We view the time we spend with our kids as a distraction from our careers.

- We pay more attention to our cars than we do to our integrity.
- We know more about our TV than we do about our spouse.
- We've turned our coworkers into pawns in our game of self-advancement.

Jesus knows that the more treasures we acquire, the greater the temptation is to tie our hearts to them. Without even realizing it, the way we see the world, like headlights that slowly dim over time, becomes distorted as we cling and grab and hoard. We walk further away from the best kind of life that Jesus wants to give us—a life of radical generosity and true contentment.

Are You a Warehouse or a Distribution Center?

In one of his letters to Timothy, the apostle Paul instructs his young apprentice in how to tackle the issues of money, possessions, and generosity in his ministry to the Christians in Ephesus. Paul writes, "Tell them to use their money to do good. They should be rich in good works and generous to those in need, always being ready to share with others."[7]

The word for *generous* here could also be translated as "ready to distribute."

I love the sense of anticipation implicit in *being ready to distribute*. It's the same feeling we get before a game or a concert: Our eyes are wide and our senses heightened because we're looking forward to what's coming. We're ready, eager, on our toes.

Paul says that we're to live with eyes wide open, ready to distribute our resources to others when the opportunity arises.

My friend Dan used to work at one of the largest UPS hubs in the country: a massive complex with a spiderweb of conveyer belts moving boxes from all over the world. It ran like clockwork. The packages that came through that facility were at that location for only a few minutes before moving on to their intended destination. The entire system was dedicated to moving packages from one location to another as quickly as possible. If a package got stuck on a shelf somewhere, that represented a failure.

I know from experience that I must constantly ask myself whether I am living generously, ready to distribute the resources that God has entrusted to me. The gravitational pull toward living like a warehouse, hoarding and stockpiling my manna, is just as strong today as it was all those years ago in the desert.

A few years ago, when Jenny and I were watching the local TV news, one of the stories was about a low-income housing community in our city that had lost air conditioning in every single apartment. This was in the middle of July, and the weather was sweltering. The broadcast showed pictures of hundreds of people, including many children, sitting in the shade outside the apartment building, fanning themselves and trying not to move so they could stay cool. The man who owned the apartment complex issued a statement that because of costs, he would not be replacing the units immediately and that the tenants would have to find alternative means of cooling their apartments.

Jenny and I had just moved into a new home, and unlike our old place, this house had central air conditioning. So we now had a used but perfectly serviceable air-conditioning window unit sitting in our basement.

I'd love to tell you that I immediately jumped up to grab that window unit and take it to those apartments. But I didn't. In fact, I fought the idea of giving it away at all.

Now, it made no sense to hold on to an air conditioner that was sitting in our basement unused and unneeded. On the other hand, my mind was flooded with *what-ifs*.

What if our central air goes out at some point?

What if the people at the apartments don't have the correct power outlet to plug it in?

What if someone in my own neighborhood needs to borrow an AC unit at some point?

The problem with *what-ifs* is that they can cause us to miss the reality of *what-is*. The *what-is* at that point was a family across town that needed air conditioning—and we had the means to help. So we finally loaded that cumbersome AC unit into our Jeep, drove over to the apartment complex, and gave it to the first family we saw sitting out on the sidewalk.

We can't get caught up in *what-ifs* when *what-is* is right in front of us. This is why generosity takes so much grit. The *what-ifs* clamor for attention in our minds, making a compelling case for why we should live like a warehouse. However, choosing to live like a distribution center, holding our possessions loosely, requires a deep reservoir of trust that God will provide everything we need.

Now, I'm not talking about being foolish or irresponsible with the gifts we've been given. I'm not talking about emptying a savings account. I'm not talking about enabling other people's destructive patterns while wrecking our own lives. I'm talking about those moments when we let our hypothetical *what-ifs* rationalize our decision to ignore a *what-is* that's right in front of us.

Radical generosity begins with a commitment to live with our eyes open, ready to distribute some of the resources that God has freely distributed to us. I promise you this: If you'll do it, your life will become richer. Richer in relationships. Richer in love. Richer in commitment to our generous God.

"Welcome Home"

A few years ago, my friend PJ volunteered at a local homeless shelter. One night, she met a man named Kevin, who shared a bit of his story with her. Kevin had been homeless for the previous thirteen years, living in abandoned buildings in Camden, New Jersey. His addictions to heroin, cocaine, and alcohol had him drowning in despair.

PJ listened to Kevin, prayed, and then did something she had never done before with any of the homeless people she had served. She gave him a business card with her name and number on it. She told Kevin to call her anytime he needed help.

For the next month and a half, PJ looked for Kevin

whenever she visited the shelter. But he was never there, and he never called her number. No one knew what had happened to him.

One night, PJ received a call from a local hospital. A staff member told her that they had admitted a patient who was in bad shape, and the only "identification" he had on him was a crumpled-up business card with her name and number.

Over the next few days, PJ visited Kevin in the hospital daily. They began to talk about where he would go once the hospital released him.

When PJ encouraged him to go into rehab, Kevin objected, saying that he had tried it before and it hadn't worked.

PJ assured him that it would be different this time because she and her husband, Ron, would walk through it with him.

Kevin agreed to go. When the hospital released him, he went straight into a forty-five-day treatment facility, and PJ and Ron were listed as his family members. They were given a list of requirements to follow if they wanted to help Kevin.

After the rehab program was over, PJ and Ron helped Kevin secure shelter for three months at a halfway house about five miles from their home. But once those three months were up, Kevin faced homelessness again. So PJ and Ron started praying that God would provide a housing solution for Kevin.

You see where this is going, don't you?

Along the way, PJ and Ron began to be confronted with the reality that following Jesus meant living with radical generosity. They began to settle into the conviction that everything they have is a gift from God, and they asked honest questions related to their responsibility in distributing those gifts to others.

That's why, on the day Kevin was released from the half-way house, they were ready to welcome him into their home. When he walked through the front door of the house, PJ and Ron embraced him and simply said, "Welcome home." Then they showed Kevin to his new room.

I can't imagine all the *what-ifs* that must have bubbled up for PJ and Ron as they considered giving generously of their resources to Kevin.

What if he steals from us?

What if he just uses us?

What if he relapses?

Those are all legitimate *what-ifs*. Any rational person would ask those same questions. And that's why the kind of generous living that Jesus invites us into will appear reckless to others.

Those *what-ifs* would be enough to make most people back down from giving generously. But not PJ and Ron. For them, all the *what-ifs* took a backseat to *what-is*. They asked all their questions, prayed for God's direction, and then applied some grit.

As Kevin settled into his new home, he started coming to church with PJ and Ron, and he began to come alive in ways he had never known were possible. But as with anyone whose eyes are just starting to adjust to the light, things were a bit blurry at first.

One night, Kevin came home and told PJ and Ron that he needed to talk to them.

"I've been lying to both of you," he said. "I haven't been sober for as long as you think I have. I've relapsed. I don't want to go back to where I was, but I need you to know that I haven't been truthful with you. I've been struggling. And I'm sorry."

At that moment, PJ and Ron realized just how far their decision to follow Jesus toward radical generosity had led them. They now realized that Kevin no longer saw them as his landlords or even as his friends. Now they were family.

PJ said to Kevin, "We'll always forgive you."

"Do I still have a room?"

"Of course you still have a room."

That night, when Kevin confessed about his relapse, PJ and Ron demonstrated the grace of God in flesh and blood. No one was getting kicked out of the house. There was no retribution. There was only a generous embrace.

That's what generosity does. It gives with no expectation of return.

But let's be completely honest. Radical generosity takes exceptional grit, because what we give may not heal the person we want to see healed. What we give may not even be appreciated. What we give may not make any discernible difference.

But sometimes it will.

I will never forget the weekend when I watched PJ, Ron, and Kevin enter our baptismal pool together. I watched the tears stream down PJ's face and mingle with the water in the pool as she heard Kevin's story of addiction and recovery read aloud to our congregation. And then she and Ron lowered Kevin into the water and baptized him.

It all started with a decision that they would live like a distribution center with the resources they had.

For you and me, living with radical generosity may not mean opening up a room in our homes to a recovering drug addict. But if we're serious about following the real Jesus, we *will* be confronted with real, tangible needs that we have the resources to meet.

The question is, are we living with eyes open, ready to distribute our resources?

Will You Grab or Give?

Generosity is not a *rule* to be followed. It isn't a nice *ethic* to live by. It's a *declaration* about the way things actually work. The world is not closed, and God's resources are not scarce or limited. They are abundant. We do not need to bow to the cynicism that says, "Hide your manna now or you may not have it in the morning." We trust that we will indeed have it in the morning. So we distribute. We bring in to give out.

Choosing to give generously is a loud, rebellious statement to the world that God can be trusted.

And no, giving generously of our money and possessions is not an easy thing to do. But as we choose to do it, we start to see the world more clearly. Our eyes are opened to the reality that it's all a gift to begin with. Our anxiety fades because we hold loosely what we have, knowing that God will always give us what we need.

CHAPTER 9

A LOVE THAT LETS GO

ONE AFTERNOON a few years ago, I answered my phone, and at first all I could hear was somebody breathing loudly. Before the first words came out of the caller's mouth, I made two assumptions: It was a man on the other end of the line, and he was angry.

"Hey, this is Jason. How are you doing?" I said.

"How am I doing? I'm mad—that's how I'm doing."

I was glad to see that my gift of discernment was fully operational.

The man was part of our church, and he wanted to talk to a pastor. For the next ten minutes, at varying decibel levels and with colorful language peppered throughout, he described just how far off the rails his daughter had gone. He said that her wedding was coming up in a couple of weeks, and he had to decide whether or not he would be there.

"Why would you not attend your own daughter's wedding?" I asked.

"Because everything about the way she's done this is wrong. She knows we don't approve of the person she's marrying. She's been living in sin this whole time, and she's not even trying to hide it from us anymore. And now she wants me to show up at this wedding as if everything's okay. No way. I'm not going to condone what she's done. What do *you* think I should do?"

I asked him whether his absence from the wedding would in any way deter his daughter from moving forward. He said it would not.

"Well, if your daughter is going to get married with or without you there, why not shock her with your love and be there? Whatever you do, don't forfeit your relationship with her in the future just so you can make a point today."

I quickly learned that he didn't really want my perspective. He just wanted my permission to go ahead with the decision he'd already made. He was convinced that his defiant act of skipping his daughter's wedding would be the most compelling way to let her know he didn't approve. My guess was that she already knew.

Before we hung up, I said, "Tell me again why you're doing this?"

"I love her too much to let her go down this road," he said.

Think about the irony of that last statement. This dad was going to sever a relationship with his daughter in the name of love. Crazy, isn't it?

And yet we do things like this all the time.

Before we judge this guy too quickly, we'd better consider our own relationships. Have you ever withdrawn from someone who let you down? Have you ever condemned, shamed, or tried to coerce people you cared about in an effort to change the way they were acting? Have you ever passive-aggressively cut someone off who wouldn't ascribe to your values? Or have you tried to justify your destructive actions under the guise of *caring for* or *loving* others?

Yeah, me too.

Maybe we need to reconsider how we love people.

Making Allowances

So far, we've covered some of the most critical areas of life and have discovered what following the real Jesus looks like in those areas. But I've saved the most important part of life—love—for last. Love is at the very core of what it means to live like Jesus and become like him. It's why Jesus said at one point, "Now I am giving you a new commandment: Love each other. Just as I have loved you, you should love each other. Your love for one another will prove to the world that you are my disciples."[1]

Don't gloss over that last sentence. It's so powerful in its simplicity.

It won't be our church attendance, how much Bible we know, our skillfully crafted evangelistic arguments, or the fish symbol on the back of our cars that will tell people we're Christians. It will be one thing and one thing alone: our love for others.

If it's true that love must take center stage in the life of anyone who wants the real Jesus and not the easy Jesus, then we should consider what it means to actually love one another.

Unfortunately, love has been sensationalized, romanticized, and dramatized in our world to the point where it is seen as little more than having sentimental feelings for someone. This may sell tickets at the movies, but we don't live in the movies. Our lives are not romantic comedies where everything works out in a rainstorm at the end. We live and love in the messy, fight-it-out, "it's complicated" real world of relationships.

The kind of love Jesus wants us to give is one that advances and grows and pursues others, no matter the circumstances. Of course, it's easy to love people when they're doing what we want and falling in line with our desires for them. But the kind of love Jesus invites us to take up is the gritty kind—the kind that keeps choosing to love even when other people's choices disappoint us, even when they don't want what we want in life, and even when they reject the desires we might have for them.

The grittiest love creates space for other people to freely be who they are. The apostle Paul tells us to "be patient with each other, making allowance for each other's faults because of your love."[2]

Love makes room.

Love allows others to make their own mistakes.

Love allows others to disagree with us.

Love allows others to pursue their own dreams.

Love allows others to discover their own faith.

Love allows others to walk their own path.

Love allows others to live their own lives.

I'm not sure there's anything that requires more grit than loving someone in that way. The real-Jesus kind of love is a love that lets go.

What's beautiful is that when we stop trying to manage the people around us, we become free to live at peace with them. Resentment and anxiety melt away as we love people for who they are, not for who we want them to be. As a result, they are free to be themselves with us, confident that we will love them as they are.

Letting Him Walk

One day, a wealthy man "came running up" to Jesus, asking how to inherit eternal life.[3] This was a guy who followed all the religious rules, yet he apparently still had a gnawing sense that there was more to life and that there was more to a relationship with God. So he approached the religious teacher who had been getting so much attention lately to see whether Jesus could put him on the right path.

Jesus told him, "Go and sell all your possessions and give the money to the poor, and you will have treasure in heaven. Then come, follow me."[4]

This guy was standing at the crossroads of easy-Jesus believership and real-Jesus followership. It was time to stop dancing around a relationship with God and to start participating in the life of God. Jesus pointed out the biggest obstacle this man had to overcome. In this case, wealth was an insurmountable barrier.

When Jesus said, "Follow me" to James and John, to Peter and Andrew, and to Matthew, they all said yes. They each threw down their nets or left the tax booth to follow him. But when Christ issued the same offer to this wealthy young man, he said no. It seemed he just couldn't give up his hoard of possessions, couldn't give up what he considered to be the good life. Instead, his "face fell, and he went away sad."[5]

This brief story is jam-packed with emotion. It starts with a man who came *running* up to Jesus. You can sense the excitement, anxiety, and hope coursing through this young man's veins. But by the end of the story, this same man is walking away with his head hung low.

But don't miss this: In the middle of the story, there is a fascinating statement made about Jesus: "Looking at the man, Jesus felt genuine love for him."[6]

This is an unusual comment. In fact, other than the references in the Gospel of John to "the disciple Jesus loved," this is one of the few times in the Gospels when Jesus is described as loving a specific person. For whatever reason, this man stirred the heart of Jesus in a particularly moving way. He loved this man and wanted him to move forward in freedom—just as he loves and wants all people who are stuck in the easy-Jesus approach to experience something so much greater.

But what did Jesus *do* as a result of his love? Did he threaten or shame the man into following him? Did he scare the man into submission? Did he beg him to reconsider? Did he nag and plead? Did he try to force him into following him?

No. He let the man walk away.

When Desires Become Demands

Think about the deep desire Jesus had to see the rich man walk a new path. Jesus knew that the direction this guy was heading wouldn't lead to life. He wanted him to turn around and take a better road.

And yet the restraint he demonstrated is a picture of love that we need to grasp. He didn't let his desires turn into demands.

Generally speaking, having desires for the good of others is a positive thing. It means we care about them and want the best for them. Even when our desires are misguided, they're usually at least well-intentioned.

Jesus didn't numb his desires, soften them, or pretend they didn't exist. Yet he also didn't press them. He didn't demand compliance from the young man. He issued an invitation: "Come, follow me." And then he let him walk away.

Evidently, loving others and allowing them the freedom

to walk their own path were not competing realities for Jesus. He didn't give the young man the freedom to walk away *in spite of* loving him; he let the man walk away *because* he loved him.

Jesus knew that if his desires became demands, the man might fall in line and do what Jesus asked; but it would not have been because the man truly wanted to. It would have been to get Jesus off his back. He would have ended up resenting Jesus for boxing him in.

So Jesus let the guy walk and kept on loving him, kept on desiring good for him.

My guess is that you have desires for the lives of people you love as well.

You desire a family member to become a Christian.

You desire that a struggling friend will wake up and get the help he or she needs.

You desire for your spouse to stop doing or saying things that undermine your relationship.

You desire for your parents or your children to stop doing *this* and start doing *that*.

There isn't necessarily anything wrong with desires like these. They may be legitimate in every way. But desires become toxic in relationships when they turn into demands. Commanding and pressuring will never work, because you can't force heart change.

Yet it's so tempting to try! So we run after the people we love, guilt them, shame them, or beg and plead with them—all in the name of love.

In many cases, if we demand that the people we love make changes, they will choose one of two responses: They will adapt and play the part for you when you're around, only to revert to living the way they want when you're not looking. Or they'll resist you altogether and run away from you farther and faster than ever. Neither option is what you're really looking for. And neither leads to a healthy relationship.

But beyond what it does to the people we love, we, too, suffer when our desires become demands. We become increasingly filled with resentment and anger toward the person who doesn't respond to our demands. We become filled with frustration. We feel impotent or turn into the sorts of tyrants we never wanted to be. Our love for the other person begins to look perilously like hate.

It is impossible for us and our relationships to be healthy when our desires for others have become demands. That's not what love is. Love "does not demand its own way."[7]

Choosing to hold back from demanding the behavior we think is in others' best interest is not only hard; it's also courageous. That's because loving others conditionally is always motivated by *fear*.

A Fistful of Fear

When our daughter was around eighteen months old, she entered a stage where she became incredibly picky about her food. (I know that's hard to imagine.)

Around this time, my parents flew in to spend some time

with us, and we all sat down for dinner one night. I barely ate any of my own food as I watched Sienna to see what she would do with the plate in front of her. After eating only a bite or two, she asked to get down from her chair.

Being the gracious parent that I was, I looked right at her and said, "No. Not until you eat at least half of everything you've been given." Sitting right in front of her was a balanced meal that perfectly filled in every section of the food pyramid we learned about in elementary school.

When she still wouldn't eat, I decided on a new tactic: I would try to reason with my toddler. Brilliant, right?

"Sienna, you need to eat these things. This is how you grow strong. This is going to help you develop."

As she stared back at me with absolutely no intention of following through on my demands, I determined that God had hardened her heart like Pharaoh's.

For the next ten minutes or so, we repeated the same conversation about two dozen times. She asked to get down, and I said no. The longer we went on, the warmer my face got. I felt something tighten up in my chest. I noticed my clenched fist was now pounding on the table, trying to bully my daughter into eating her food.

My parents had been patiently watching me the entire time, but when I began to pound the table, my dad spoke up and asked me a question that cut to the chase.

"Jason, why are you so worked up that Sienna isn't eating?"

At the moment, it seemed like a ridiculous question. He had been a parent of young children, so he knew how important it was to ensure that they were healthy and thriving. I responded immediately with a lie about how concerned I was for Sienna's well-being.

"I want the best for her," I said. "It's my job to teach her how to take care of herself in order to be healthy."

My dad just stared at me. Sienna must have inherited that trick from him.

After a few seconds of silence, the truth finally made its way from my heart to my mouth: "I'm worked up because I'm afraid. I'm afraid she won't be healthy. I'm afraid she'll develop bad habits. I'm just afraid."

Love doesn't pound its fist on the table to coerce a small child. Only fear does that. And love and fear can't live in the same house. There are just too many irreconcilable differences. As the apostle John says, "Perfect love drives out fear."[8]

When we give in to fear, we convince ourselves that we can't be content until other people live up to our desires. As one writer observes, "When you cling, what you offer the other is not love but a chain by which both you and your beloved are bound. Love can only exist in freedom."[9]

My dad's simple question brought into the open that my fears for my daughter were robbing me of the capacity to simply love her in the moment. By resting my own happiness on whether she made the choices I wanted her to make, I found myself clinging. Instead of offering Sienna my unconditional love, I offered her a chain. And it did her no good. It didn't do me much good either.

The opposite of love isn't hate—it's fear. Our fears have a corrosive effect on our capacity to truly love others.

I wish I could say that my foolishness with Sienna was the first and last time I've let fear guide me in my relationships with my loved ones. But the truth is that, out of a fear of failure, I've used people around me in my own pursuit of success. For years, I was afraid that my wife would find out I'm a sham, so I kept her at a safe distance and refused to let her get too close. And I've been afraid again and again in so many different ways.

Let's face it—fear is exhausting. But we don't have to live that way, because love *drives out* fear.

Loving Who They Are

Nothing puts flesh and blood on Jesus in our world more than loving others for who they are, not just loving who we want them to be.

Isn't that the plot of the gospel? God's relentless love toward us is demonstrated by his sacrifice while we were still an absolute mess. The apostle Paul says that Christ died for us "while we were still sinners."[10] He freely gave his love for us even though we wanted nothing to do with him. There were no conditions to his love, no fine print. And even if there were never any change in our lives, not even an ounce of acknowledgment of his love, he would still love us the same way.

We need to ask ourselves a difficult question: Can we, will we, walk the same path as Jesus and love the people around us *while they are still sinners?* If we're serious about following Jesus by loving others, it means loving the people around us for who they are *today*, not just loving who we want them to become *someday*. It may mean letting go of our dreams and desires for them so that we can experience the wonder of who they are *right now*.

I know that allowing someone you love to walk away in freedom is a painful proposition—especially when "freedom" means they may walk down a destructive path. We may see our loved ones go down the dark road of addiction, compulsion, and self-destruction. We may see their lives implode before our very eyes. When that happens, our hearts are filled with grief and pain because we know the hope and life that could be theirs if they would just wake up, turn around, and accept the love of God.

I understand how difficult this can be. I've had far too many people who are close to me walk through complicated, painful relationships. It's tough to stand by and watch. But the alternative—demanding that people change—is an even more miserable way to live.

We want to experience peace in our relationships, the kind of peace that leads to our enjoyment of those we love. We can experience that kind of peace, but only by offering freedom.

Here's what I suggest for relationships where you've been making demands and producing only frustration: Entrust those people to God. You're not abandoning them by doing this. You're just giving up responsibility for change in their lives.

Pray a prayer like this: "God, I trust you with [name here]. They are yours to change, and they are mine to love. Amen."

Pray that one thousand times a day if you have to. Then step back and watch what happens.

Letting Go and Getting Back

My friends Jay and Karen are on their second marriage—to each other.

The first time, they hadn't been married for long when Jay began to drink. At first, it was no big deal—a drink or two with dinner. But as the months went on, his drinking became more and more frequent, and it began to put a strain on their young marriage. In the middle of all that tension, they found out that Karen was pregnant.

After the birth of their daughter, Jay's drinking got even heavier. Now it was causing serious problems for their family life. In her angrier moments, Karen would yell at Jay about his behavior, hoping that her words would convince him to stop. In her more rational moments, she calmly pleaded with him to get help for his out-of-control drinking. None of it did any good, so she finally asked him to leave.

He moved out, and a divorce ensued.

In the middle of all this, Karen came to our church for the first time. She found a group of women who loved her and her daughter. They spent time talking about the difficult days that Karen was going through.

Even though Karen still loved Jay and was sorry about the

loss of her marriage, her eyes became more and more open to the reality that demanding that he change could never have worked. She finally acknowledged that she did not have the power to reach inside his heart and transform him. Instead, she began to consider what it might look like to love Jay just as he was, not as she wanted him to be. At first, that simply meant trusting God with Jay and praying for him. But she continued to hope that their relationship might change for the better at some point.

During this time, Jay came face to face with his own brokenness. He finally confronted the destructive wake he had created behind him. He was alone, hurting, and desperate for healing that only God could provide. When he found that healing in Jesus, he walked away from his addiction and began the journey toward grace. Part of that journey involved the difficult task of reconciling relationships he had wrecked.

One day, he called Karen and asked whether they could meet at a local park. She agreed. When they got together, Jay told her about the work that Jesus was doing in his heart. He asked for her forgiveness, and Karen forgave him.

They kept meeting casually for a while, until finally they felt safe enough to start dating again. As they continued to spend time together, their love for each other was revived, and exactly six years after their first wedding date, they got married a second time. Today, their marriage is thriving, and they have become premarital mentors at our church, leading engaged couples toward what it looks like to love in ways that allow freedom for the other person.

Does every story end this way? Absolutely not. I could list countless other examples of people I know who never saw their spouse turn around, never saw their child step out of addiction, never saw their friends find hope in Christ.

But here's the thing: How it ends isn't the point. We don't make the tough choice to love others so that we'll get the happily-ever-after ending we want. Ultimately, loving others isn't about the effect it has on *them*. It's about the effect it has on *us*. Loving in ways that bring freedom to others is part of what it means to live a rich and satisfying life. In giving others their freedom, we experience our own freedom from resentment and anxiety.

With Karen and Jay, they won each other back long before they were remarried. When she stopped demanding that Jay change as a condition for her love, she began to experience an unprecedented peace in the relationship. As a result, Jay experienced what it meant to be loved for who he was, not for who Karen wanted him to be.

Their remarriage was a result of the freedom that Karen had already experienced when she stopped trying to control Jay and let him walk his own path. Even if they had not remarried, she could still love him, pray for him, and help him—not out of fear but out of her freedom.

Pastor Peter Scazzero says, "The critical issue on the journey with God is not 'Am I happy?' but 'Am I free? Am I growing in the freedom God gave me?'"[11]

When it comes to the people you love, are you free?

Have your desires become demands, leading you toward

growing resentment and anger because those around you won't live up to your demands?

Are there people you need to love enough to let go?

If you will release them from your expectations of who they should be, you may win them back in a brand-new way, experiencing them for who they really are. As a result, you will discover the peace that can come only in a relationship built on freedom.

CHAPTER 10

SECOND NATURE

IF YOU'VE NEVER HEARD of Frank Nelson Cole, you're missing out. He was a mathematician who gave a presentation titled "On the Factorization of Large Numbers" at the American Mathematical Society's annual convention in 1903. In that one-hour presentation, Cole accomplished something that no other mathematician had been able to do.

Yes, I know we're talking about math, but this will be good—I promise. Besides, you've made it this far, so why bail out now?

If you haven't completely blocked out your middle-school years, you probably remember learning something about prime numbers. A prime number is any number that can be divided only by itself and the number one. So, for instance, three is a prime number. So is five. So is seven. So is 7,919.

During the seventeenth century, a French philosopher/ monk/theologian named Marin Mersenne became consumed with prime numbers. He set out to devise a formula to determine whether a number is prime or not. It's easy to figure out that three is a prime number, but what about 1,336,723,092? Eventually, Mersenne had what he thought was a workable formula, which he ran all the way out to $2^{67} - 1$. (That's two multiplied by itself sixty-seven times, and then minus one.) That number became known as the Mersenne prime, and for hundreds of years (long before calculators or computers came along) mathematicians tried their best to prove whether the famous Mersenne prime was really a prime number.

When it came time for Frank Nelson Cole's presentation at the mathematician's convention, he walked to the front of the room, where there were two chalkboards waiting. Without saying a word, he started writing a number on one of the chalkboards. When he was finished, the mathematicians in the room all recognized the twenty-one-digit number as the Mersenne prime. (In case you're wondering, it's 147,573,952,589,676,412,927.)

Again without saying a word, Cole walked over to the second chalkboard and wrote

$$761,838,257,287$$
$$\times\ 193,707,721$$

For the next hour, he multiplied the two numbers by hand— in complete silence.

When he reached the final digit of his calculation, the number equaled the Mersenne prime, thus proving that the Mersenne prime was not a prime number after all.

As you might imagine, the roomful of mathematicians went crazy!

Cole dropped his piece of chalk and walked back to his seat, having not said a word the entire time—because Frank Nelson Cole is The Man.

When someone asked him later how long it had taken him to figure out the equation to disprove the Mersenne prime, Cole replied, "It took me three years of Sundays."[1]

In other words, for 156 Sundays, Cole had committed himself to the painstaking task of writing down two large numbers and then multiplying them to see whether the answer matched the Mersenne prime. When it didn't, he started over using different numbers.

He did this every Sunday for three years.

When you look up the word *grit* in the dictionary, it should have a picture of Frank Nelson Cole.

When I first heard about Cole, I couldn't help but wonder, *What if he had stopped after the third Sunday? Or the seventy-sixth Sunday? Or the 155th?*

What if he had chosen to hide behind excuses?

"It's too hard."

"I've got better things to do with my time."

"There are others who are more qualified than I am to do this."

Sure, Cole was educated and had the tools he needed to do what he did. But what's fascinating to me is that, when asked how he had accomplished something so incredible, he didn't mention any of that. What he talked about was his willingness to keep at it. He talked about how he woke up every Sunday and recommitted himself to the task at hand. Ultimately, that perseverance, focus, and sheer grit got him where he wanted to go.

That's how life-change happens.

Jesus invites us to follow him, again and again—156 times over and beyond. As we wake up each morning and make the decision to follow him again, we begin to see that the life we once found so challenging has become second nature and that our hearts have been transformed.

Seven Tough Choices . . . and More

We've looked at several key areas of life where the toughest decisions lead to the greatest outcomes. Let's bust a quick review:

1. When we've been wronged

When others have wronged us, the easy thing to do is enter into a cycle of recycled revenge, demanding payment for the wrong that's been done to us. The tough decision is to absorb the debt by forgiving the other person. When we make that choice, we find freedom as a result, and we're able to move forward again in life.

2. When we encounter needs

When we come across someone who is hurting and in need, the easy thing is to feel pity and to pray for God to meet the need. The tough decision is to convert our compassion into action that helps the person in need. When we do this, we partner with God in his restorative work in the world, bringing a glimpse of heaven to earth.

3. When we've been handed pain

Every time we experience loss, illness, failure, or some other kind of pain, we'll be tempted to numb it or run from it. Those are the easy options. But if we choose the toughest path instead, by owning our pain and offering our stories for the healing of others, God can redeem our pain by transforming it into good.

4. How we seek intimacy

Every day, the world shows us the easy path of sexuality as a means of selfish, short-term pleasure. Jesus shows us the difficult path of sexuality as a special part of our larger pursuit of real connectedness and intimacy. This genuine connection is what we really crave deep down. By reining in our impulses in order to pursue intimacy, we find the kind of connection we've been longing for.

5. Where our ambition leads us

We all choose how we will use our energy, our position, our authority, and our power. The easy choice is to "lord it over others" while building our own personal kingdoms. But if we're ready to make the tougher choice, we will leverage the best of ourselves in humble service to others. As a result of humbly lowering ourselves to lift up others, we can experience a life of true greatness.

6. How we use the resources we've been given

When we're deciding what to do with our money and possessions, the easy thing is to keep stockpiling it to ensure greater degrees of security. The tougher choice is to live as "distribution centers," ready to give generously from the resources we've been given. This tough decision is the one that leads to contentment and satisfaction.

7. How we love others in freedom

It seems easier to try to control the people we love by demanding that they live up to our desires and expectations for them. It's much harder to allow them to go their own way and love them anyway. But only unconditional love will produce lives of peace and contentment and will give us a chance to maintain and enhance our relationships.

As we have explored these tough choices, the purpose hasn't been to convince you to agree in principle with any of them. The purpose is to promote *action*. Agreeing in principle allows us to remain as passive spectators to the life that Jesus is inviting us into. The call of the real Jesus is for us to *move* and *participate* in these new ways of being.

Here's another dose of reality: For the rest of your life, Jesus will continually ask you to follow him. Nothing will be tougher than taking him up on that invitation. But if you are faithful in your response, you will be able to look back one day at remarkable progress. In fact, I believe that you will see an acceleration in the pace of your progress over time. That's because summoning the grit required to follow Jesus into his way of life will become second nature—an ingrained habit—for you. You'll follow him more consistently and with less hesitation, and you'll experience more and more of the fullness of life that Jesus has promised.

Here's the most amazing thing of all: This second nature that you will acquire over time is really the nature of Christ *in you*. Tough decision after tough decision, grit upon grit, day after day, you will see yourself becoming more like Jesus. The process won't be fully completed until you stand before Jesus face to face. But even now you can undergo a stunning transformation as "the Lord—who is the Spirit—makes us more and more like him as we are changed into his glorious image."[2]

Want it? Keep following.

Again

I love the scene at the end of the Gospel of John where the resurrected Jesus is having breakfast with his disciples beside the Sea of Galilee. With the light of dawn streaming from the east over the water, it must have seemed to the disciples as if they were standing on the shoreline of the future, looking forward. And in so many ways, they were.

Yet the reunion on the beach that morning was also charged with tension. That tension revolved around Peter, the most outspoken disciple, who had been the first to declare that Jesus was the Messiah yet who had also, on the night of Jesus' arrest, denied that he even knew Jesus. Peter's relationship with Jesus was filled with both passionate commitment and broken promises.

I can relate. Perhaps you can too. What Peter needed most at that moment was the same thing we all need most: a fresh start, a chance to choose Jesus all over again.

That's why the simple invitation that Jesus offered to Peter on the beach that day is so stirring to me.

Despite Peter's denials, despite Peter's failure to follow when the pressure was most intense, Jesus seemed intently focused on offering Peter a chance to start over. He didn't dig into the backstory and demand an explanation for why Peter had denied him. He didn't shame Peter or show disappointment in him. He simply said, "Follow me."[3]

Isn't that interesting?

As I mentioned in chapter 1, some of the first words that Jesus spoke to Peter were "follow me."[4] And now here, at the end of their earthly relationship, Jesus says the same thing: "Follow me."

It's the same invitation that Jesus whispers into the hearts of everyone who is willing to listen. It's the invitation that you and I woke up to today and that we will wake up to tomorrow: "Follow me."

"Yes, I know about that failure. Follow me."

"Yes, I know you didn't follow me yesterday. But today? Follow me."

"Yes, I know your life is difficult and challenging. You're weary. I understand. Follow me. I will give you everything you need."

If Jesus didn't give up on a man who had given up on him, he's not giving up on you, either!

Although we don't know what Peter *said* after Jesus' final call to follow him, we do know by his actions that his heart answered with a *yes*. We know it because we have the book of Acts, which records how Peter boldly preached the gospel and rallied the church in the weeks and months after Jesus left the earth. The very same Peter who was cowering in a courtyard and lying to a little girl about knowing Jesus became a shining example of gritty faithfulness to God.

By your actions you will give your own response to Jesus' ongoing call to follow him. I hope that you, like Peter, will experience a new infusion of Spirit-led courage and that you will boldly make the difficult choice to follow the real Jesus because you know the kind of life he's leading you toward.

How does it look from where you're standing on the shoreline of your future?

Are you willing to say yes again today to the invitation to follow the real Jesus?

Are you willing to put into practice the kind of life you most long for?

Practice Makes Progress

In a 2004 article titled "Live More Musically," journalist Andy Crouch explores the differences between purchasing music and practicing music, which he compares to "playing a CD [or] playing a fugue."[5] One of his main points is that we experience different levels of satisfaction with music we've learned to play through long hours of sacrifice than with music we've merely purchased.

If you want a good example of how fast your satisfaction wears off with music you have purchased, go back through your iTunes library and count how many albums you "just had to have" that you haven't listened to in years.

Embarrassing, isn't it?

Part of the reason for this is that the music we purchase delivers almost all of its satisfaction up front. In other words, we'll never be happier with a product we've purchased than when we use it for the first time. After that, our satisfaction level tends to go down. For some songs and artists, it will be a frighteningly quick downward slide on the satisfaction scale. (Any boy bands coming to mind right now?)

But when we learn to play a musical instrument, the satisfaction curve moves in the opposite direction. During the early stages, there is little enjoyment. (Not just for us, but even more so for those who have to endure our attempts to blow air through a brass instrument or draw a bow across strings.) But if we make the choice to grit it out and keep practicing, in time something beautiful will happen. What at first were discordant noises will eventually become distinguishable notes. And those notes will eventually become phrases, melody, music.

In a separate article on a similar theme, Andy Crouch comments on the power of practice over purchase:

> Practices, done consistently over time, expand our own capacities in fundamental and irreversible ways. Practice the violin for an hour a day, for twenty years, and at the end you will be able to do things, to create things, you were completely unable to do and create before. Listen to recorded violin music for the same amount of time, and while you may by the end have a pretty complete mental grasp of the violin repertoire, you will be just as helpless with an actual violin as you were twenty years earlier. . . . But when we practice, we change.[6]

Back when we were stuck in an easy-Jesus approach, we all wanted the change without any of the practice. We wanted to play one right note and then walk away thinking we'd mastered the music.

For a long time, we had been hearing about the kind of life that Jesus was calling us into, but we had merely listened to it as we listen to good music. We had never actually picked up an instrument and tried to play; we had never tried to practice what we heard. And while others felt free to join in and play along with the music, we stayed in the spectator seats, admiring from afar and frustrated that others seemed able to live in ways we couldn't.

I've had people tell me that they just can't forgive someone. Or they can't hold their tongue. Or they can't give generously of their resources until X, Y, and Z happens. But the truth is, they could do all of these things if they were willing to practice. They may not be very good at it yet, but if they dig in and keep practicing those ways, over time they'll learn to play the music.

We may think that some people are just naturally more forgiving, trusting, or patient. They're not, just as there is no one for whom humility, compassion, or generosity comes naturally. There are only those who have made the difficult, gritty decision to *practice* particular ways of living until those ways become ingrained in the very fabric of their character. No one can microwave greatness. There are no virtuosos at the first piano lesson. It takes time and practice—grit applied again and again.

Jesus desires for us to become so skilled at living in rhythm with his ways that the things that once were so difficult become second nature.

When we keep making the tough decisions to step into his way of life, we discover new realities about ourselves and about God. As we experience God's provision in giving us all the desire and power we need to move forward, we grow in our ability to trust him. We create new habits of faithfulness, like grooves worn in a malleable surface. And when we're faced with a choice between an easy, wrong option and a tough, right one, we make the tough, right decision because those habits have become our default. Our whole way of operating changes.

Jesus wants to transform every fiber of our being. But we have to choose to say yes to that transformative work.

In medieval Europe, Benedictine monks wore clothing made of simple cloth: unpretentious, functional, and probably a bit uncomfortable. When a new monk entered the order, one of the first things he did was give up his old clothes and receive his new habit. But the old clothes weren't thrown away, as you might expect. The monks hung the old clothes right next to the new ones. Each and every day, when it was time for the Benedictine brothers to clothe themselves for the day ahead, there was a choice right in front of them: old clothes or new?[7]

We have the same choice to make every day: old ways or new? If we patiently and consistently practice living the life of Jesus, before we know it the clothes that once seemed a bit uncomfortable will begin to fit just fine. And if we wear them long enough—choosing to open the closet and put on the new clothes day after day—it will soon be the old clothes that don't feel comfortable anymore.

And it won't be because the clothes have changed.

It will be because *we* have changed.

Today It Was Different

My friend Lauren is one of the grittiest followers of Jesus I know. A few years ago, she gave up on the easy Jesus. She had *believed* in Jesus for a long time, but now she found herself stirred to begin *following* him. Over the past few years, this new commitment to follow the real Jesus and make the tough choices has transformed her life step by step.

When Lauren was young, she lived under a barrage of physical and emotional abuse from her brother. For years, she carried the pain secretly—running from it or finding ways to numb it when she couldn't run. But this approach had led her down a dark path of shame and bitterness. She realized that she would have to make some tough decisions if she wanted to follow the real Jesus and allow him to redeem her past. Slowly but surely, she began to own her story and offer it to others by sharing it.

Not everyone was comfortable with this. Her parents didn't believe what she said about her brother, and this led to a growing divide within the family. What grieved Lauren the most was that her parents had never been even remotely interested in anything spiritual, and now she wondered whether she had jeopardized her opportunity to have any influence in their lives.

Still, she woke up each day and recommitted herself to following the real Jesus, accepting whatever tough choices he might ask her to make that day. Over time, she began making small decisions to work through forgiveness with her brother, and she began to confront what it might look like to live generously and compassionately with him.

One day during the holidays, as Lauren was driving home after church, she started thinking about the gifts she would get for her family. Then it hit her. What, if anything, would she get for the brother who had wronged her? The immediate answer was simple: *nothing*. But then her new nature as a follower of Jesus kicked in, and she saw that there might be an opportunity for generosity and compassion right in front of her.

Later that day, she e-mailed me and told me what she had done:

> Immediately after leaving church today, I went to my brother's favorite restaurant and bought him a $20 gift card. It may not seem like much, but handing over a gift card to someone who has wrecked my life took every last ounce of forgiveness I possess. I cried the whole way home. But I also know who I am and who Jesus is inviting me to be. I am going to be the person who shows honor no matter how challenging it may be.

Did she feel like making that tough decision? No. She cried the whole way home. But she knew from experience that feelings are not a prerequisite for following. She refused to allow her feelings to overrule her decision to follow through on the tough choice that Jesus was inviting her to make. As a result, she has discovered that following the real Jesus brings *life* on the other side, no matter how wrenching the decision may be at the moment.

A few months later, Lauren's grandfather passed away. At

the funeral, as the family settled into their seats in the front row, Lauren's brother sat down next to her. It was the first time they had been in such close proximity since Lauren had brought into the open all the ways he had hurt her.

Shortly after the funeral, she told me, "A couple of months ago, sitting next to my brother would've sent me into a full-blown panic attack. But today it was different. Today I was actually okay."

Today it was different.

That is a profound statement of transformation.

Why was it different?

Because *she* was different.

Over time, Lauren has been transformed by the countless gritty decisions she's made to follow Jesus, even when nothing in her wanted to. Each choice moved her further down the road toward the life that can only be found on the other side of following the real Jesus.

Lauren would be the first to tell you that it hasn't been easy. But easiness isn't the point. What matters most in life is what's *best*. When we pursue what's best, the difficulty becomes a means to a greater end—the fullness of life that Jesus has for us.

If you're a Christian, you didn't sign up for the easy life. You signed up for the good life. And sometimes *good* demands something of us. Or as F. Scott Fitzgerald once said, "Nothing any good isn't hard."[8]

Of course following the real Jesus is not going to be easy.

Why would we expect it to be? The greatest treasures in life are often the ones we work and sweat and bleed for.

If you make music, the songs you create have value to you because of all the work you put into them, not because of any monetary gain you might receive.

If you're an athlete, the countless hours of sweat, blood, and tears that you've invested in your sport are what make it valuable to you.

If you're a parent, the home you've created has value because of the relentless love you've poured into the relationships formed in that space.

We inherently attach value to the things we've worked the hardest to accomplish. And on the other side of all that effort, perseverance, and pain, we expect it all to be worth it.

By choosing to follow the real Jesus, you've chosen a path that will be difficult, demanding, and trying at times. But you've chosen it with the belief, the faith, that in the end this way of life is both good and best. On the basis of that faith, you move forward, putting one obedient foot in front of the other. After you've done that again and again and again, you'll find yourself, as Lauren did, sitting in a seat you never thought you'd sit in, giving gifts you never thought you'd give, forgiving people who don't deserve it and haven't asked for it, and becoming the person you never thought you'd become. Over time, you will realize that what was once difficult has become second nature.

You'll find yourself saying, "Today it was different."

The Best Kind of Sore

Following the real Jesus never ceases to be challenging. But when it becomes second nature, we at least know what to expect, and we have confidence that we have the tenacity and the capacity to follow through and make the right decisions—today, tomorrow, and every day afterward.

Recently, I decided to exercise with my "I make marathons look easy" wife. When I work out, I usually do it by myself. But this time I thought it would be nice to share the time with Jenny. I'm not ashamed to tell you that I couldn't even finish the workout. (Actually, that's a lie—there's definitely some shame in telling you that!)

At one point, I asked if the workout was almost over.

"We're only in the warm-up," Jenny said.

I wish that were a joke. Let's just say I struggled.

But as I lay on the floor in exhaustion at various times during the workout, I noticed something. Jenny wasn't struggling as I was. The workout was demanding for her, too. It required focus, energy, and effort. But she was able to do things I couldn't do.

You know why, don't you?

She had been doing this particular training program for several weeks. She had struggled the first time, as I had. But now her body had gotten past the initial fatigue, and her muscles were beginning to develop "memory." In other words, what had started out being difficult was now becoming more natural. This, in turn, allowed her to push herself even harder.

In all honesty, following the real Jesus will leave you feeling a bit sore every time you have to exert yourself. Why wouldn't it? We're using "muscles" we aren't used to putting into motion. But if you're brave enough to let your obedience muscles be taxed—brave enough to trust that if you keep practicing the ways of Jesus with everything you have, there is fullness of life on the other side—you'll find that decisions that were once so difficult have become second nature. And you'll find yourself doing things you didn't think you could do.

The soreness you feel is no longer a pain that makes you question whether you should continue. It now reminds you that you're getting stronger and that your capacity is growing. It's the best kind of soreness you could have.

Honoring your spouse when things are going well builds the relationship muscles you will need to honor him or her when it feels as if your marriage is barely hanging on.

Respecting your parents when it's relatively easy builds the muscles you'll need to respect them when it's most difficult.

Practice mercy now so that you'll be able to give it when it's needed most.

Practice forgiving small offenses now so that you'll be ready to forgive the big ones when they come.

Practice humility in small ways now so that when it's really needed, you'll respond naturally.

If you choose to follow Jesus again and again, choosing to take on his yoke countless times over, it will become an ingrained habit before you know it. At first, it may seem difficult and unnatural to leave the easy Jesus behind. But the more you begin to live like the real Jesus, the more natural it will become and the more you will share in his glory.

My greatest prayer and hope for you is that no easy Jesus will ever satisfy you again.

From this point forward, only the real Jesus will.

Contagious

Can I share one last thought with you?

When you have developed the habit of faithfully following Jesus even in the hard things, people will begin to notice. They'll see what it means to go beyond just believing in Jesus to another way of living in relationship with him. Their eyes will be opened to the possibility of their own transformation because they have witnessed yours. Perhaps they, too, have been disappointed in their life of faith—discouraged, frustrated, or bored—and haven't known what to do about that disappointment. But now, because of your grit and because of the grace of God displayed in your life, they've caught a glimpse of new possibilities. Before long, they may be following the real Jesus right there along with you.

Do you remember my friend Lauren? After her grandfather's funeral, she returned home with her mom and dad. As they were standing in the kitchen, her mom said to her, "It seems like you and your brother were okay today."

Lauren replied, "What he did to me will always hurt. But yes, I'm done fighting with him about it, because I forgive him."

Lauren's mom just looked at her without saying anything. So Lauren went upstairs to her room.

A few minutes later, her mom walked into her room and asked, "Do you think Dad and I could come to church with you sometime?"

And that's exactly what happened. The very next weekend, for the first time ever, they came with Lauren to church.

They didn't ask to go to church with Lauren because they were bored and needed something to do on a Sunday morning. They were compelled by the change they had seen in Lauren and wanted to know what she had found. They wanted the same kind of life transformation they had seen in her since she had decided to follow the real Jesus.

Transformation is contagious like that.

The people in your life aren't expecting you to articulate every nuance of what you believe. In fact, most of them aren't even asking, "*How* do you follow Jesus?" Rather, they are asking, "How do *you* follow Jesus?"

You can answer the first question in an e-mail. Or in a book. But you can only answer the second question by living your life in front of them. By waking up again tomorrow and making choice after gritty choice to take Jesus up on his invitation to follow him.

Fullness of life awaits on the other side of those tough choices.

Go grab it.

ACKNOWLEDGMENTS

Sienna and Silas: Thank you for the sacrifices you've made along the way that have allowed me the time and space to write. You guys are my greatest gift, and my love for you has no limits. Let's keep chasing after Jesus together!

Mom and Dad: You have always pushed me to pursue Jesus with all I have. Thank you for never letting me settle.

My family in the Southeast and the Middle East: We may be spread out, but my roots are tied to each of you. And I wouldn't want it any other way. I love you guys.

PawPaw: You gave me tenacity.

MeeMaw: You gave me joy.

Grandmama: You gave me safety.

Granddaddy: You showed me that anyone can change.

Garber Family: An initial thought needs a quiet space to evolve into a full-blown idea. Your cabin provided that space for me early on. Thanks for your generosity.

Nolts and Graybills: Thank you for always asking, "How's it going?"

Kara G: Though it seems like a lifetime ago, you helped get this whole thing rolling. I'm pretty sure it was the Wilbur Buds and Isaac's that sealed the deal.

Lesa S: Even before the first word was written, you let me know you were in my corner. Not everyone can offer skillful critique and encouragement at the same time. You have that gift, and it helped carry me through. And . . . RTR!

Dave D, Matt P, Amy S, Michael F: This book has your fingerprints all over it. It is better in every way because of you.

Adam H: To say that I couldn't have done this without you is no cliché. The behind-the-scenes expertise you've provided has been invaluable. Thank you.

David A: I do not take it for granted that for the past fifteen years you've entrusted me with an incredible privilege: to stand up, open the Bible, and unpack what it means for us to follow Jesus. It's hard to express how grateful I am to have you as my pastor, leader, and friend. Everyone should be so lucky.

Don G: Most of what I have is because someone took a chance on me. Thank you for reaching out and taking a risk. I wouldn't want to be on this ride with anyone else.

Kyle I: Thanks for believing that I have something to say.

Eric S: You helped clarify the things I couldn't, all the while breathing new life into me and into this book. Thank you.

Jan LH and the Tyndale Momentum team: When you promised me early on that you were going to make me work,

I had no clue how serious you were. And I am incredibly grateful that you followed through on that promise.

Doug W, Phil H, Harley A: You gave me vision, inspiration, and fire in my belly to dream big about what the church could be in this world. Thank you for launching me.

Kevin B: Thank you for listening to my ideas and affirming that they actually make sense. If only everyone could have a friend like you.

Jon B and Chris S: Yes, I'm dedicating chapter 9 to you. Thank you for breaking the speed limit.

The BRC team: Ministry is so much more fun when you get to do it with people you love. Thanks for having my back.

Life Groupies: There's no better way to spend a Wednesday night than with you. You've always made it safe for me to be me. That's a gift I treasure.

LCBC: I cannot imagine a more impassioned movement of Jesus followers than you. You have shown me countless times over what it looks like to follow Jesus into the unknown. May the movement never stop moving!

Future Islands, Abigail Washburn, Jack White, Elevation Worship, Radiohead, RJD2, Jeff Buckley, Johnny Cash, Robert Johnson: Thanks for the soundtrack to write to.

Nick S: Thank you for returning the Tide to our rightful place of dominance.

NOTES

CHAPTER 1: JESUS ON A SHELF
1. John 10:10
2. Eugene H. Peterson, *Run with the Horses: The Quest for Life at Its Best*, second edition (Downers Grove, IL: InterVarsity, 2009), 50.

CHAPTER 2: GRIT
1. Matthew 4:19, 8:22, 9:9, 10:38, 16:24, 19:21
2. John 12:26
3. Luke 9:57-62
4. For further reading on the idea of "believing in," see Leon Morris, *The Gospel according to John*, (Grand Rapids, MI: Eerdmans, 1995), 88, 296. In referring to what it means to "believe in" Jesus, Morris observes, "This is more than simple credence. It is not believing that what he says is true, but trusting him as a person. It is believing 'in' or 'on' him. The Greek expression used here is found in the papyri . . . and it seems to be linked with the idea of possession. If the New Testament retains anything of this usage, the expression will convey the additional thought that when we believe, we yield ourselves up to be possessed by him in whom we believe."
5. Colossians 2:6
6. Galatians 6:8, 9
7. Colossians 2:7
8. Angela Lee Duckworth, "The Key to Success? Grit," TED, April 2013, http://www.ted.com/talks/angela_lee_duckworth_the_key_to_success _grit?language=en.
9. Peterson, *Run with the Horses*, 161.

10. Dallas Willard, *The Great Omission: Reclaiming Jesus's Essential Teachings on Discipleship* (New York: HarperCollins, 2006), 80. Italics in the original.
11. Matthew 11:28-30
12. John 6:60, NIV. Italics added.
13. John 6:66, NIV
14. Philippians 2:12-13

CHAPTER 3: ABSORBING THE DEBT
1. Luke 11:4
2. Matthew 6:14-15. See also Ephesians 4:32; Colossians 3:13.
3. Luke 6:27-28
4. Coldplay, "Death and All His Friends," *Viva La Vida or Death and All His Friends* (Parlophone, 2008).
5. Luke 6:37, NIV.
6. Romans 5:10
7. Matthew 6:15; Mark 11:26
8. Psalm 103:8-12
9. Luke 6:36, NIV
10. Miroslav Volf, *The End of Memory: Remembering Rightly in a Violent World* (Grand Rapids, MI: Eerdmans, 2006), 9.

CHAPTER 4: SKIN IN THE GAME
1. Ecclesiastes 4:1
2. Matthew 6:10
3. Helen H. Lemmel, "Turn Your Eyes upon Jesus" (1922). Public domain.
4. Matthew 20:30, 32-34, NIV
5. Mark 1:40-41
6. Luke 7:12-14
7. John 1:14, MSG
8. Amos 5:21-24
9. *God Grew Tired of Us*, directed by Christopher Quinn and Tommy Walker (National Geographic Films, 2006).
10. Ibid.

CHAPTER 5: WE ALL BLEED
1. Matthew 26:30
2. Psalm 118:5-7. Italics added.
3. Frederick Buechner, *Secrets in the Dark: A Life in Sermons* (San Francisco: HarperCollins, 2006), 212.
4. John 20:19-20. Italics added.

5. John 20:25
6. John 20:27-28
7. Anne Lamott, Facebook post, August 24, 2015, http://www.facebook
   .com/AnneLamott/posts/720031968126449.

CHAPTER 6: GETTING NAKED ON THAT OLD BURGUNDY CARPET

1. Genesis 1:10, 12, 18, 21, 25, 31
2. Genesis 4:1, KJV. Italics added.
3. Genesis 2:24
4. See Deuteronomy 6:4, NASB, NIV.
5. Genesis 2:25
6. C. S. Lewis, *Mere Christianity* (San Francisco: HarperCollins, 2001), 105.
7. Timothy Keller with Kathy Keller, *The Meaning of Marriage: Facing the Complexities of Commitment with the Wisdom of God* (New York: Dutton, 2011), 226–227. Italics in the original.
8. Matthew 5:27
9. Matthew 5:27-28
10. Matthew 5:29
11. Ephesians 5:25

CHAPTER 7: LOWERING AND LIFTING

1. Psalm 8:3-4
2. Psalm 8:5. Italics added.
3. Ephesians 2:10
4. Psalm 8:6
5. See Genesis 1:28.
6. See Genesis 2:15.
7. Anne Rice, *Christ the Lord: The Road to Cana* (New York: Anchor, 2011), 97.
8. Mark 10:37. Italics added.
9. Mark 10:42-43
10. Jeremiah 2:11, NASB
11. Mark 10:43-44
12. Mark 10:45

CHAPTER 8: ENOUGH

1. Exodus 16:15-16. Italics added.
2. Exodus 16:17-18
3. Exodus 16:20
4. See Luke 12:33.

5. Matthew 6:21
6. Matthew 6:22-23
7. 1 Timothy 6:18

CHAPTER 9: A LOVE THAT LETS GO
1. John 13:34-35
2. Ephesians 4:2
3. Mark 10:17
4. Mark 10:21
5. Mark 10:22
6. Mark 10:21
7. 1 Corinthians 13:5
8. 1 John 4:18, NIV
9. Anthony de Mello, *The Way to Love: Meditations for Life* (New York: Random House, 1992), 26.
10. Romans 5:8. Italics added.
11. Peter Scazzero, *Emotionally Healthy Spirituality* (Grand Rapids, MI: Zondervan, 2006), 132.

CHAPTER 10: SECOND NATURE
1. Ira Glass interview with Paul Hoffman, "So Crazy It Just Might Work," *This American Life*, November 11, 2011, http://www.thisamericanlife .org/radio-archives/episode/450/transcript.
2. 2 Corinthians 3:18
3. John 21:19, 22
4. See Matthew 4:19.
5. Andy Crouch, "Live More Musically: The Difference Between Christian Practice and a Starbucks Purchase," *Christianity Today*, August 1, 2004, http://www.christianitytoday.com/ct/2004/august/20.54.html.
6. Andy Crouch, "From Purchases to Practices," *Q: Ideas for the Common Good*, http://208.106.253.109/essays/from-purchases-to-practices. aspx?page=3. Accessed September 16, 2016.
7. M. Craig Barnes, *When God Interrupts: Finding New Life through Unwanted Change* (Downers Grove, IL: InterVarsity, 1996), 55.
8. Matthew J. Bruccoli, ed., *F. Scott Fitzgerald: A Life In Letters* (New York: Macmillan, 1994), 314.

About the Author

JASON IS TEACHING PASTOR AT LCBC (Lives Changed By Christ) Church, a thriving church with locations throughout Pennsylvania. Through speaking and writing, Jason has influenced thousands of people to pursue Jesus with passion. He gets fired up about finding new and compelling ways to make the message of Christ relevant to people's everyday lives.

During his free time, you'll find Jason drinking coffee, getting in a quick run, watching the University of Alabama beat other teams in football, or listening to all things rock-and-roll. He lives, works, and writes outside of Philadelphia with his wife, Jenny, and their two children, Sienna and Silas.